Copyright © 2025 Dominique M. McMillan & Dr. DuBois Teddy McMillan

All rights reserved. No part of this book may be reproduced, distributed, or transmitted in any form by any means, or stored in a database or retrieval system, without prior written permission from the publisher.

Published by QuestVersity

The World's Easiest Book label is owned by QuestVersity

Visit our website at www.questversity.com

First published in 2022

Some of the characters and events portrayed in this book are fictitious. Any similarity to real persons, living or dead, is coincidental and not intended by the author.

ISBN: 978-0-9769623-3-5

Printed in the United States of America

The World's Easiest Book on Why Social Emotional Learning Matters (Revised)

a practical guide for parents, teachers, caretakers, coaches, recreational workers, or anyone who works with children

Dominique M. McMillan
&
Dr. DuBois Teddy McMillan

Dedication

This book is dedicated to my first best friend, Diane Thompson. She loved to tell others, "I had her to spoil her" and she did just that! Thank you mommy for all the sacrifices, those seen and unseen. I know you made many sacrifices raising me as a single mom, it was just me and you! However, you never let me see or feel our struggle. You fought through the pain and despair of some really hard times but you demonstrated what a mom should do and be for her children, and for that I am forever grateful. You taught me how to be resilient, kind, respectful, true to who I am, the importance of family, and most of all, how to be a woman of God. I wish we could lay in your bed and stare at the ceiling one more night and talk about everything! I would say, "Thank you for loving me the way you did!" You will forever hold a special place in my heart that will never go away.

Psalms 127:3 reads, "Children are a gift from the Lord; they are a reward from Him." To my three greatest gifts from God. *Imani* - thank you for loving me unconditionally as we figured out together how I could be your mother and your friend. You are strong, caring and independent. Don't ever change! *Moon* - thank you for being you and helping me to live my life on my terms and my way. You keep me calm, centered and fly. *Sir* - you are and will forever be my beautiful baby boy that helped me see life through a new lens. You continue to show me that life is full of adventures and how dreams can become a reality. Keep soaring son!

To the love of my life, my husband, my King and my best friend since the ripe age of 18. You've always accepted me for who I am and encouraged me to use my gift from God to help others realize their potential, discover what makes them happy, and live more purposeful lives. Thank you for being patient and co-writing this book with me. You are my motivation and strength. I love you babe!

Finally, to my grandmother who I affectionately call, "Gran". Thank you for being such a blessing to me and my family. You have always believed in me, shining like a bright star in my life. Rest in peace to my uncle Kenny, who you took care of for many years and demonstrated what unconditional love looks like as a parent. We love and miss you Uncle. Lucille M. Adams, you are the BEST!

In memory of my sweet mother-in-love, Eloise McMillan. You loved me and I loved you dearly. We had a special bond. From our trips to the store, doing your hair weekly, to taking you to the doctor, we built an unforgettable bond that I will always treasure.

Introduction

Hey There, I'm Dominique...

I am so excited that you decided to purchase this book. I love to work with parents, educators, community members, coaches, counselors or anyone who works with children. Together, we can make the world a better place.

So, *Why Does Social Emotional Learning(SEL) Matter?* It matters because these skills are important in helping students experience success in school and in life. This book will take you through each of the five (5) social-emotional competences: self-awareness, self-management, social awareness, responsible decision-making and relationship skills. We will give you tools, tips and strategies throughout this journey, including a tool that we call the **TREC Method**. My husband and I developed this principle-based strategy to help us work through tough situations. We will dive more into the TREC Method in Chapter 2 of the book.

Social-Emotional Learning is the process of developing the self-awareness, self-control, and interpersonal skills that are critical for success in school, work, and the social world. Through SEL, children learn to recognize what's happening inside of them and become aware of their emotions, which helps them deal with impulsive behaviors. It helps them stop, take a breath, and think about a situation before acting. Children learn to identify others' emotions and perspectives, which helps them develop empathy and show compassion towards others. SEL also helps children learn to problem-solve in a peaceful way and communicate constructively about what they need or want.

One of the things I've learned in my 27 plus years of parenting my own children, doing workshops, and working as a parenting specialist, is that we need clear strategies to help us communicate effectively and build rapport and respect for others.

This book is extremely interactive and geared to help you develop a deeper understanding of SEL. So lets get started on this journey together. Happy reading!

Chapter 1

Exploring the Whole-Child Model

Academic success only tells one part of the story.

The purpose of this chapter is to help you become familiar with the Whole-Child model so that you can understand its importance in supporting the cognitive, social, and emotional growth of children.

...what you will be able to do at the end of this chapter:

- Identify the 5 Tenets of the World-Child.
- Examine the 5 Tenets of the Whole-Child as a comprehensive approach to youth development.
- Create an infographic that incorporates the 5 Tenets of the Whole-Child concept and articulate how the infographic can be used to inform others.

...materials needed for this chapter:

- Jane and her Mother Video *(go to www.questversity.com >> Why Social Emotional Learning Matters link)*

Children thrive when they are loved, feel safe, supported, and valued by loving adults.

Whole-Child: Introduction

All children want to feel safe, loved and supported. That's one of our primary roles as parents, or anyone who works with children. We spend an enormous amount of our time trying to manage our own personal lives in addition to nurturing and caring for our children. While attempting to care for ourselves and dealing with the many problems that life throws at us, we still have the responsibility of raising our children regardless of how stressful or unstable our personal and work lives might be. As we all know, the needs of children can differ from child to child and take on various layers of complication. This makes our roles more complex and it becomes even more important for us to develop strategies, and have tools and resources to become more active in our roles as parents, coaches, counselors, teachers, mentors, etc.

In this chapter, we will explore the Whole-Child concept. We will take a look at a common scenario that many of us may have encountered as parents and think about how we might prepare ourselves better if confronted with similar situations in the future by using a principle-based strategy called TREC (*thinking-respect-empathy-compassion*) designed by the authors of this book. You will learn about TREC later in the chapter, but for now, view or read the story of Jane and her mother. To view the scene, go to www.questversity.com and click on the **Chapter 1** link under the book's title, ***The World's Easiest Book on Why Social Emotional Learning Matters.***

Go to www.questversity.com
or

Read the story on the next pages

Jane and Her Mother

FADE IN:

INT. NEAT LIVING ROOM - DAY

JANE, 12 years old, is SITTING at a small desk with a notebook stretched out before her and she's struggling to solve math problems. OVER THE SHOULDER CLOSE-UP of the NOTEBOOK and we see JANE's HANDS, and she moving a pencil across the page.

> JANE
> (Mumbling to herself)
> Take away seven...divide by three...

She lets off a loud SIGH.

> This is just too hard. I don't know any of this. This is soooo stupid.

MEDIUM SHOT OF JANE. She SLAMS the pencil down on the desk. The SQUEAKING DOOR opens. Jane's mother, SUZIE, steps in.

> JANE
> (cheerfully)
> Hi ma!

JANE smiles.

> SUZIE
> (dejected)
> Hi.

WIDE SHOT of SUZIE as she walks directly to the table, PICKS UP MAIL, and starts reading. JANE watches on with the notebook in her hand. SUZIE never looks in JANE's direction.

> JANE
> (Hesitates)

>   Ma, can you help me...

SUZIE stops, thrusts her arms to her side, and lets off a deep SIGH.

>   SUZIE
>   What is it, Jane?

Jane stands with a BLANK FACE, lowers her head.

>   SUZIE (CONT.)
>   You know I'm busy Jane. I just
>   can't right now. You know what
>   I'm dealing with.

Jane turns, walks back to her chair, and sits down. Suzie watches her.

>   SUZIE
>   I'll cook something later. I need
>   to get some rest right now. We'll
>   talk later.

OPTION #1

SUZIE sees that Jane is obviously affected by her actions. She turns back to Jane.

>   SUZIE
>   Dear, look...I'm sorry. I was
>   so...so tied up with the mail that
>   I didn't see how your day went. I
>   apologize.

Jane smiles.

>   JANE
>   It's okay mom. I understand. I
>   realize you are going through a
>   lot.

>   SUZIE
>   No...no...no. That's not okay. I
>   have to get better at this. I want
>   to know how you are doing. So, how
>   was your day?

            The two SMILE.

    OPTION #2

        SUZIE enters her bedroom and shuts the door. Jane goes back
    to struggling with the math problems.

    OPTION #3

        JANE huffs.

                        JANE
                I need help with my math. Can you
                help me?

                        SUZIE
                Math? You know I'm not good at
                math. Did you ask your teacher for
                help?

                        JANE
                Well, I did but I didn't really
                grasp it in class. Now, it's like
                I forgot everything.

                        SUZIE
                Well, do your best. I just can't
                help you right now. Like I said,
                I have to get some rest and
                there's so much I have to deal
                with.

We will discuss this story in more depth later in the chapter

Jane's situation is no different than many children I personally know, read about, or have personal interactions with. Life can be hard for both children and their parents. Single parenting, domestic violence, having a shortage of money, employment challenges, and a host of other problems can all contribute to anxiety and other mental health related challenges that impact a child's ability to learn. According to Jimenez et al (2016), children often struggle in school due to adverse experiences they face at home, school, and in their communities. Thousands of school-age children are considered at-risk of experiencing social problems such as substance and domestic abuse, poverty, homelessness, incarceration or failing in school.

What we didn't know about Jane's story is her parents are on the verge of getting a divorce and her mother is trying to maintain a sense of normalcy so that Jane's life is not totally impacted by choices Jane has no control over. This new information might change how we view Jane's mother and it might explain how Options #2 and #3 might be typical responses considering the circumstances. As someone who has children and also works with children, we must be able to accept and understand that children come to us with a multitude of experiences and circumstances and we must be open to exploring matters more before casting judgment.

Gone are the days when education was solely focused on cognitive development and academic success, a child's social-emotional needs must also be addressed in order for a child to be well-rounded and prepared for school and life after school. No doubt, being a child in today's world is more difficult today than it was when I was a child. There's a strong argument that today's children have the pressures of social media, cyber-bullying, social acceptability, and a host of other potential influencers.

> What is happening in Jane's life?
>
> Is this normal?
>
> What do you think can be done to help?

The problems that most children face today are bigger than what most traditional school settings had to grapple with in the past. These problems range from academic challenges to social and mental challenges, or many cases, a combination of all of these. Therefore, the approach to helping children must be comprehensive and well thought out. We must look at everything a child faces in order to best serve each child's unique needs. So, we need to look at the **Whole Child**. Every aspect of a child's development needs to be considered in order to help build healthy young people to become healthy, responsible adults.

The 21st century student must learn to compete in today's global marketplace. Students need to be creative, be able to problem-solve, work in a team environment, collaborate, and live in an ever-changing world. In addition, students also have to be able to deal with and handle real issues and adverse experiences that many school-age children face such as divorce, poverty, family and community violence, mental illness, health issues and other serious circumstances to become prepared to achieve success in life.

- *Only 29% felt that school created a caring, nurturing environment*
- *Less than 50% developed critical social competencies*
- *30% of high school students had engaged in multiple high risk behaviors*

Data from learningpolicyinstitute.org - (educatiing the Whole-Child)

The only way that we can can truly prepare a child in today's world is to look closely at all of these factors. With the complexities in the type of problems children face today, we must broaden our lens and be willing to engage in tough conversations, explore research-based data on what works and what is not yet been proven to work, and adjust practices to meet those needs. We can no longer depend on standardized test scores and college acceptances only in determining whether a child is really prepared for the next phase of life.

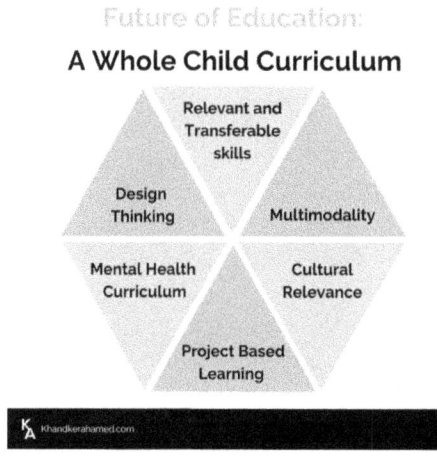

In 2004, the Association for Supervision and Curriculum Development (ASCD) introduced the Whole Child approach, recognizing that for children to thrive in today's competitive world, they must develop the ability to adapt swiftly to change and think critically.

When I interviewed for a position as Assistant Program Director for a Science, Technology, Engineering and Mathematics (STEM) program for 3rd through 12th graders, I shared in my interview that one of my goals, if given the position, would be to expose students from under-represented groups to the various opportunities in STEM in order "to prepare them for jobs that didn't exist at the time." That was over 20 years ago. Today, our children need to be even more well-rounded in their learning in order to be marketable and employable in a competitive job market. With this type of approach to learning, we are preparing students to be successful not only academically, but socially and emotionally.

This approach looks at all the factors that affect a child's development and eventual success. The goal is long-term success instead of short-term achievement. What I mean by this is that we need everyone to be involved. Students like Jane must receive adequate attention and support to develop the skills necessary to navigate life's unexpected challenges effectively. From their preschool years to young adulthood, students need the skills and attitudes to understand and manage their emotions. **Now, let's get back to Jane's story.**

Three Major Takeaways from Jane's Story

1. Jane is like many other children across this country

2. Jane has little to no control over her circumstances

3. Jane is at-risk of experiencing failure

■ ■ ■

One of the key benefits of *experiential learning* is that you can reflect on an experience and apply what you have learned to new experiences. Here, I want you to reflect on Jane's experience and list things that resonate with you. Later, you will be engaged in a scenario-based activity where you will apply what you have learned.

Activity #1: List Your Takeaways from Jane's Story

Activity #2: Discuss in Groups

1. What are some problems children might face at home that can impact their ability to perform at their highest potential in school? Jot a few responses below and discuss with someone at your table, breakout room, or home.

2. What type of services do you think are offered when a "Whole Child" approach is implemented? Discuss with your partner and write your answers below.

Tenets of the Whole-Child Model

The goal of the ASCD's approach is to create a system that ensures that all relationships, practices, and policies created for children considers the child's health, safety, engagement in learning and connection to the community, systems of supports, and the level of challenge in the academic experience. Each component must work together to achieve the goal of a whole-child approach in education.

If we fail to take a comprehensive approach, we fail to adequately prepare students for the ever-changing world.

> 1. Each student enters school **healthy** and learns about and practices a healthy lifestyle
>
> 2. Each student learns in an environment that is physically and emotionally **safe** for students and adults
>
> 3. Each student is actively **engaged** in learning and is connected to the school and broader community
>
> 4. Each student has access to personalized learning and is **supported** by qualified, caring adults
>
> 5. Each student is **challenged** academically and prepared for success in college or further study and for employment and participation in a global environment (Whole Child Education, 2022)

Figure 1.2 presents a list of critical features that teachers, schools, and communities must provide to satisfy the Five Tenets of the Whole-Child approach.

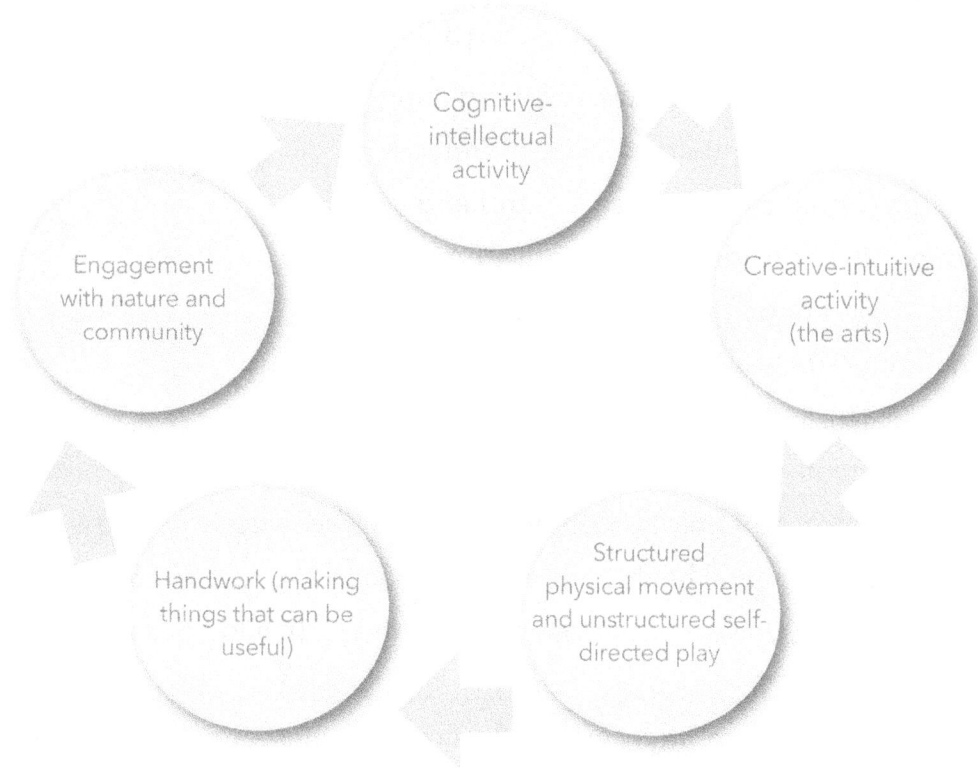

Source: Association for Supervision and Curriculum Development, 2007

As we explore the Whole-Child concept in detail, we will be giving you recommended activities that can be done in school, at home, or in a recreational environment to help you support healthy and uplifting interactions with children. For now, let's get into the Five Tenets of the Whole-Child.

TENET 1: STUDENTS MUST BE HEALTHY

Research shows that students are better prepared to succeed academically when they are physically and emotionally healthy (Alvarez-Bueno et al., 2017; Kuhnhausen et al., 2013; Sneck et al., 2019). This is especially important when we see the glaring statistics that over one-third of U.S. children are overweight (Centers for Disease Control and Prevention, 2019). Additionally, about 11 million children live in hunger and struggle to meet the recommended daily nutritional needs (Feeding America, 2019). In the same vein, one-in-six children experience mental health illness (Cree et al., 2016) in the United States, and only half of these children received treatment from a mental health professional, according to a 2016 study conducted by the University of Michigan Health Lab (Child Focus, 2022).

Children suffering from any physical health struggles or psychiatric disorders have higher risks of failing in school, dropping out, and suffering long-term effects (Breslau, 2010; Kuhnhausen et al., 2013; Sneck et al., 2019). Therefore, when children have better health, and nutritional support as well as active physical programs, they can concentrate more, achieve higher test scores, miss fewer days of school and perform better academically (Basch, 2010; Chinaveh et al., 2010; Grotan et al., 2019; Wassenaar et al., 2019). While this data is difficult to accept, we can't avoid it and must think of ways to work collectively to bring resources together to support children's overall health.

Activity #3: Reflection (Individual)

1. In terms of health, what are some ways that health can specifically affect a child's ability to reach their full potential?

2. What are some ways that schools, families, and communities can support healthy living for children?

TENET 2: STUDENTS MUST BE SAFE

Research shows that when certain psychological needs are met, a child feels safe in school. This can lead to a more healthy well-being, increased engagement, and improved academic outcomes (Twemlow, 2002). In the same light, research also shows that students exhibiting disruptive behaviors and decreased classroom engagement can adversely affect performance (American Association of University Women, 2011). Students who are victims of crime or violence in school may experience adjustment difficulties, loneliness and are more prone to become truant, engage in violent behaviors, have poor academic performance, and drop out of school (Duszka, 2015).

Thoughts:

Feeling safe in school translates into higher academic achievement, increased student well-being, and greater engagement, according to numerous studies (Lacoe, 2013; Kutsyuruba et al., 2015). Children who feel safe are better able to concentrate on their studies and connect with their classmates and are more likely to attend school more consistently. According to a research study conducted by the Concordia University (2016), when students feel safe, they will be more attentive and efficient in class and show fewer symptoms of depression because they are engaged in the work and actually enjoying themselves. This brings me to a well known motivational theory in the area of psychology that was created by Abraham Maslow, an American psychologist, who believed that we as humans have innate needs that must be satisfied. For example, when an individual has their basic physiological needs met such as food, water, warmth, and shelter, they are now prepared to seek "safety" along the hierarchy on their way to the final stage, which is self-actualization. As you can see, safety needs are at the second level on this hierarchy and critical to an individual's progression to higher levels on the hierarchy. Self-fulfillment needs are more complex and aren't necessarily acquired in a linear fashion.

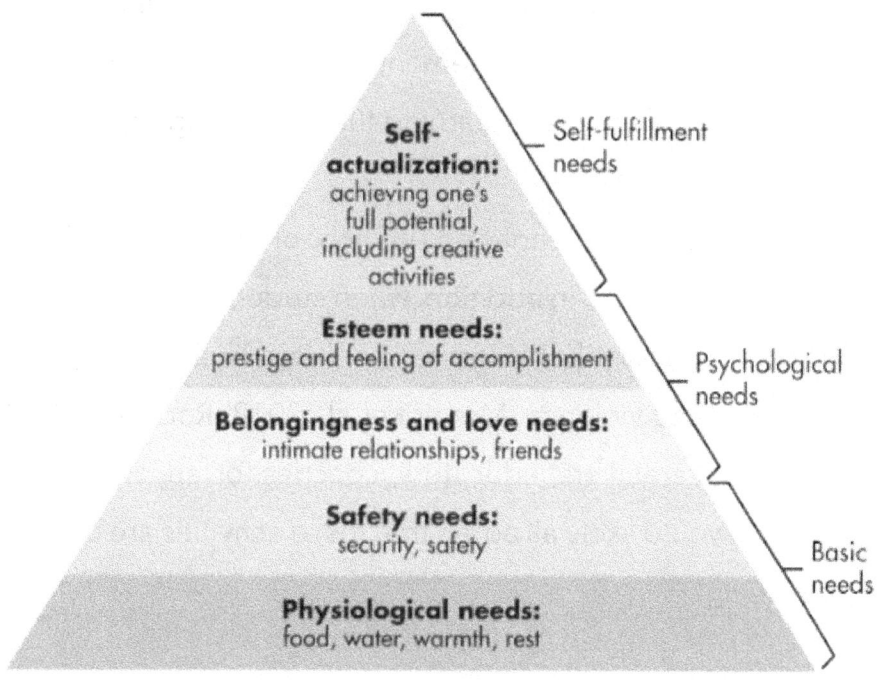

Source: www.simplypsychology.com

TENET 3: STUDENTS MUST BE ENGAGED

According to a National Survey in January 2018, one in three teens are bored most of the time in school (Bitsko et al., 2018). This poses a serious barrier that we must address because optimal learning takes place when students are motivated to learn (DePaoli et al., 2018). This is especially important because, as students get older, their level of interest in school decreases and peaks sometime in elementary school. Many middle and high school teachers struggle to make learning fun and engaging.

When students are more engaged in school it impacts their school performance (Payne, 2018). In addition, when students feel valued in school, they exhibit positive social behaviors and are less likely to engage in drug use, sexual activity and violence (Moreira et al., 2018; Rodriguez-Fernandez, 2017). As parents, caretakers, educators, coaches, or anyone else working with children, we would likely all agree that these activities are detrimental to a child's well-being.

Engagement is not limited to the classroom. We want students to be connected to school activities such as clubs and teams, involved in civic action and community service, and connected to the community in general and able to utilize resources that can assist them in navigating life.

Activity #4: Safety Needs and Engagement (Individual or Group)

1. Conduct a quick Internet search on Maslow's Hierarchy of Needs. Pay close attention to "safety" needs and answer the question below.

Why do you think the fulfillment of safety needs are so critical to a child's ability and motivation to learn?

2. List two positive benefits of student engagement in the learning process, civic action, and personal growth.

TENET 4: STUDENTS MUST BE SUPPORTED

The environment in which students learn affects the performance of the student. According to Kweon et al (2012), children need an environment that is safe, healthy, stimulating, and supportive to grow and learn because they spend about eight hours at school, which largely shapes and reshapes their intellectual ability. Research shows that when the learning environment is supportive, it helps the students develop positive attitudes towards school, increases their expectations of success, and boosts their academic motivation and engagement (Ekanem et al., 2011). This is important for increasing student achievement outcomes.

Thoughts:

Psychologists believe the environment can affect the quality of one's critical thinking and how much a child can learn in school (Duckworth et al., 2012). Other studies show that supportive environments can help students achieve positive emotional and social development, and this could lead to increases in critical thinking and resiliency. Other works of literature also confirm that when students are motivated and engaged in learning, it lowers emotional distress, and susceptibility to other dangerous activity such as substance abuse and violence (Balaguru et al., 2013; Kerr et al., 2013; Gould et al., 2018). This is not to say this will eliminate these problems, but having the right supports in place can help organizations address these issues.

TENET 5: STUDENTS MUST BE CHALLENGED

As a 21st Century learner, real success in school, college or in the workplace can be achieved with effective communication, problem-solving skills, and higher-level thinking as well as an understanding of the world and its people (Cassidy et al., 2018). This involves being fully engaged in a rigorous curriculum geared towards preparing students for a competitive world. According to Jamye & Gallayanee (2016), 80 percent of Americans believe high school graduates should be prepared for college and careers.

Thoughts:

However, many high school graduates do not have the knowledge and skills to make them competitive in the current job market. A large number of high school graduates have to take remedial courses because they have not mastered foundational skills that are needed to succeed at the collegiate level. In addition, about 13 percent of high school students indicated that they considered dropping out of school because their schoolwork was too easy. Nearly 50 percent of students in the same study stated that they were not adequately challenged in school (Yazzie-Mintz, 2010). The bottom line is, the work must be interesting and challenging in order to maximize learning.

Activity #5: Supporting and Challenging Students

1. Name two ways in which schools, community-based organizations, or other recreational/sport clubs might provide special support for a child.

2. In the space below, define the word **Rigor** in your own words.

3. If a child in your program is not challenged or engaged in rigorous processes, how can that affect their personal outcomes? Please explain in the box below.

Activity #6: Fishbone Group Activity

INSTRUCTIONS:

Step 1: Get in a group of 4 to 5

Step 2: Discuss your reflections from the 5 Tenets of the Whole-Child

Step 3: Draw an image of a Fishbone similar to the picture below

Step 4: Choose one of the tenets

Step 5: On the head of the fish, write one of the Five Tenets

Step 6: On the left side of the skeleton, write potential issues related to the tenet written on the head of the fish

Step 7: For each issue on the left, write solutions on the right for each issue in the left

Non-Cognitive Skills: Are They Important?

As implied earlier, the essential skills every student must develop for academic success and success in life are problem-solving skills, communication, and critical thinking. These skills are categorized as non-cognitive skills and may further include social skills, persistence, creativity, self-control, and a host of other skills.

Thoughts:

The term non-cognitive represents the patterns of feelings, thoughts and behavior which may develop throughout our lives and are dynamic traits allowing us to succeed in our homes, workplaces, public entities and other societal contexts. This ultimately contributes to the growth and development of society as a whole (Garcia & Weiss, 2016). Research findings have linked non-cognitive skills to positive life outcomes in various ways such as positive health indicators, success at work, productivity, and achievement in career and in school (Garcia, 2014; Duckworth & Yeager, 2015 Lippman et al., 2015).

Non-cognitive skills can also reduce behavior-related problems because it presents students with a grounded background that goes beyond the limitations of the school's curriculum (Heckman & Kautz, 2012). Research also pays attention to the fact that the best time to develop positive non-cognitive skill developments for long-term economic benefits is through pre-school

and early years intervention (Heckman et al., 2013). We must create learning approaches that not only build skills, but also attitude and behaviors that support short and long-term success in academics and in life. The whole-child approach provides a comprehensive learning approach that supports the growth and development of cognitive, non-cognitive, social and emotional skills in a healthy, safe, engaging, supportive, and challenging environment.

As a former senior consultant with one of the leading non-profit organizations in Early Childhood Education (ECE), we provided leadership, guidance, and professional development to early education programs, ensuring best practices were implemented in developing the whole-child. I will be sharing much of that knowledge and many of the strategies in the upcoming chapters, along with tips that have helped me as a parent and facilitator.

Activity #7: Non-Cognitive Skills

1. In the space below, think of other non-cognitive skills that are not listed in the discussion bubble on the previous page and write them in the boxes. If you can't think of three, write at a least one.

2. As you think about non-cognitive skills, think of skills that you might possess personally. Enter them in the spaces below. You can use skills from the discussion bubble or those listed in Question 1.

CHAPTER 1 CHECKUP

1. The Whole-Child approach focuses on providing adequate support for a child's academic success.   True ☐   False ☐

2. Which of the following is not one of the tenets of the Whole-Child Model?
    - ☐ Safety
    - ☐ Health
    - ☐ Communication
    - ☐ Engagement in school and community
    - ☐ Challenging academic experience

3. Non-cognitive skills cover a broad range of personal attributes that might include motivation, character, teamwork, and other traits.
    True ☐   False ☐

4. One of the tenets of the Whole-Child approach is **safety**. In order to fulfill this component, schools and community spaces must ensure that the environment is emotionally and _____ safe for children and adults at all times.

5. The following activities below are examples of connecting to the school and broader community:
    - ☐ Volunteering for a school campus cleanup
    - ☐ Participating in a community service project
    - ☐ Attending a youth conference on a current topic
    - ☐ All of the above

CHAPTER PROJECT: INFOGRAPHIC MOCKUP

Project: Infographic Mockup
Time: 45 minutes
Delivery: Groups of 4 or 5. If taking the class online or at home, you can work on this independently.

INSTRUCTIONS:

In this project, you are going to be working with a group of 4 to 5 team members. You are tasked with brainstorming ideas for an infographic that you can use to inform others on the Whole-Child concept.

You must incorporate the 5 Tenets of the Whole-Child in your design. You should be as creative as possible when designing and developing your infographic, but you do not have to create a digital infographic.

You will share your mock-up design with the group at the end of this activity. In chapter 6, you will have time to develop the five components of SEL into a digital infographic.

DO THIS: create a mockup (sketch) of an infographic that incorporates the 5 tenets of the Whole-Child. You can sketch it on a sheet of paper.

Chapter 2

Self-Awareness

Real change and understanding starts with understanding ourselves.

The purpose of this chapter is to explore self-awareness and understand how it helps individuals develop a sense of how to recognize their own strengths, weaknesses, confidence, thoughts and emotions, and how these things influence our attitudes, moods, and behaviors.

...what you will be able to do at the end of this chapter:

- engage in conversations with children to help them identify and label their emotions.
- understand how self-confidence and self-efficacy influence one's emotional state.
- understand how growth mindset affect one's outlook.
- use the TREC Method to create an activity with your child, relative, student, or player, that helps you understand them better.

...materials needed for this chapter:

- no additional materials are needed for this chapter

Knowing who you are and being able to label your feelings are two of the greatest assets afforded to us.

Introduction: Self-Awareness

Self-awareness is all about knowing who you are, being able to identify your emotions, knowing your strengths and weaknesses, and being aware of how each of these influence your behavior. Our thoughts have a huge influence on how we act, and we oftentimes act upon the emotions we're feeling at any given time. Self-Awareness is a concept that we can use to look at our thoughts and feelings objectively so that we can better understand ourselves. This will help us know what our personal strengths and weaknesses are, our level of self-confidence, and our personal belief in our ability to complete a particular task (self-efficacy). In this chapter, we will explore self-awareness through dialogue with others, short case studies, and a scenario-based activity where you will make decisions on how to respond in a life-like situation.

At the end of the chapter, you will be more aware of how self-awareness can help you better support youth by implementing strategies to help them build self-awareness.

Angie's Ballet All-Stars (Part 1)

Getting her dancers to commit to doing ankle strengthening exercises brings collective groans from Angie's advanced level youth ballet class. On different occasions, she had asked them the reasons for their aversion to the warmup exercises, which she knows is necessary for them to get better at balancing their bodies and reducing the likelihood of injury. Additionally, Angie had done these same exercises as a kid and knows how valuable they were in helping her make it to the Youth National Competition in New York, where she won a scholarship and had a successful career working as a professional ballerina in Canada. Some of the kids talked about how "hard" the exercises were and how they made their feet hurt. Others talked about "how much they don't really need to do the exercises to do well in competitions." Considering the team had won three straight regional competitions, there was obviously something contributing to their success. To combat this problem, Angie began most classes by sharing real-life stories about the importance of each exercise, especially in relation to how they helped her get better and prepared for her career. The additional ten minutes in pep-talk pushed the ending time back and she started getting complaints from parents about how the additional minutes was cutting into their kids' homework and dinner time.

Other background information:

- Angie has been running the school for five years and has one of the most popular schools in the area. The closest school of her school's caliber is 20 miles away.

- A few parents have complained in the past about her brash demeanor and how she comes off as "stand-offish" but they know she's a great instructor because of how well her teams do in regional and national competitions.

During a final practice before a regional competition, Angie became infuriated when her dancers came to practice and complained yet again about the exercises. In response, Angie told each ballerina to "exit the floor until you are ready to respect the art." A few parents were sitting in the stands and recognized that Angie's actions were a bit over the top, and had noticed her demeanor gradually changing over the course of the season. Angie couldn't help but overhear a comment from a parent as she escorted the dancers off the floor. "She doesn't care about them." The parent's words stung Angie at the core, but she knew a quick reaction would only make things worse.

Activity #1: Angie's Dilemma

1. What emotion is Angie feeling in this moment? Why is she feeling this way?

2. What is the parents' major dilemma here?

3. Beyond what we already know about this case, what do you think Angie's rationale might be for telling the dancers to leave the floor?

What is Self-Awareness?

When we have a good sense of what we are thinking and what we are feeling, we have a better opportunity to control the behaviors that usually come as a result of these thoughts and feelings. Being able to identify these thoughts and emotions make us more self-aware. Self-awareness helps us have better control of outcomes because they give us an opportunity to capture thoughts and label emotions before committing some action. There are some actions that are involuntary of course, like when you accidently jam your toe on the edge of a table. "Ouch!" That hurts even thinking about it. But, when you think about the response, there wasn't really enough time to think about what an appropriate response might be, right? Or, was it?

Think about this for a second. Let's say for some strange reason you have your shoes off while you are at work. Better yet, let's pretend you were recently hired at a company and you went over to a colleague's house for a holiday celebration and they had plush, light carpet in their house and they had already sent out an email telling all employees who attend the party that they must take their shoes off before entering the house. Whew! I know that was long, but stay with me. Yes, I've actually attended several parties like this. But, let's say you take your shoes off and as you're walking into the living where everyone is seated and having a jolly good time, you jam your toe against a tall bar chair. Would your response be the same as when you are at home by yourself?

Activity #2: Reflection (Individual)

What would your response be at the party?

What would be your response at home?

Maybe this example was a little exaggerated, but you get my point. I could just see myself using a lot more words from my personal word bank that are in a special category when I'm at home versus in a setting around people I'm just getting to know. But, the real conversation here is about being able to recognize how you are feeling at any given time. In most cases, when we are talking about having self-awareness, we aren't referring to involuntary reactions to physical pain. What we are talking about is being able to label your emotions, being able to think about an appropriate response, before taking some action. Being aware of our emotions and being able to identity them helps us to assess our emotions more accurately in order to avoid conflict with others and build better relationships.

According to the Collaborative for Academic, Social, and Emotional Learning (CASEL), here are some ways to demonstrate a strong sense of self-awareness and purpose:

- Identifying emotions
- Recognizing strengths and areas of growth
- Growth mindset
- Self-confidence
- Demonstrating self-efficacy (CASEL, 2022)

So, after we take another look at Angie's action to demand the dancers to exit the floor, what are two things you think Angie should've considered?

Activity #3: Reflection (Group or Individual)

Consideration #1:

Consideration #2:

Think about the last time you got angry and did something out of anger. What additional feelings were you experiencing?

Do you think that additional emotion made matters worse? Please explain.

IDENTIFYING EMOTIONS

One of the first steps in resolving conflict constructively is to be able to identify the emotions that you are experiencing. This is a critical step in owning the emotion and thinking of ways to regulate the emotion by channeling the energy in ways that minimize conflict.

In the chart below, the faces represent a broad range of emotions that we might feel at any given time. From the personal experience you shared from **Activity #3** on the previous page, circle the emotion(s) that you felt in that moment. This is an important step in being able to regulate emotions.

Feeling Faces chart - trails to wellness. (n.d.). Retrieved January 20, 2022, from https://storage.trailstowellness.org/trails-2/resources/feeling-faces-chart.pdf

After you are able to name the emotion, it's always great practice to take a moment to simply quiet your mind so that multiple things aren't running through your mind at the same time. During this "thinking" stage, you should think of one or two alternative paths that you might take in order to meet your personal objectives and the interests of those who contributed to why you are feeling the way you are. For example, I remember something precious was stolen from me as a kid. Of course, I was angry. But, deep down inside, there was a full range of emotions such as being hurt, feeling betrayed, empty, and worried, that were all working simultaneously and made it difficult for me to control my emotions. As a result, I felt helpless and simply cried. This incident had triggered so many feeling that it was difficult for me to gather myself. It is in these moments that I realized I have to be able to unravel and unpack each of these emotions one-by-one in order to go to a better place. So, taking a seat, controlling my breathing, and thinking about other things that may have happened to the item, actually took my mind off of the individual who I thought may have taken it. While reflecting, I began to feel less betrayed because I didn't even consider this person a friend in the first place. Though this didn't take away my anger, I no longer felt betrayed.

Let's see what Angie did next.

Angie's Ballet All-Stars (Part 2)

Angie called her former coach later that night and shared the experience with her. It felt good to talk to someone about her dilemma, because in some strange way she felt responsible for the whole ordeal and wanted to make things better. Her coach, now retired, shared a few things with Angie that helped her see a different perspective. She asked Angie to do two things. First, describe the emotion she felt when her ballerinas did not do the exercises. Secondly, she asked her to share what she felt were her strengths and weaknesses. It didn't take long for her to respond to her strengths and weaknesses, that was easy. "I know a lot about how to become a successful ballerina, but at times I can be hard, and I know I have to work on that," she said. Her former coach then asked her to think about how she could work on her weaknesses and turn them into strengths. Angie didn't quite understand what she meant by that. The coach explained in more detail. "Well, you expressed that you are hard on your ballerina's, right?" she confirmed. Angie answered, then explained more about how she felt they wanted to take shortcuts to success and not put in the hard work. Right then, Angie realized she had answered the first question. When the ballerina's didn't do the exercises it made her "angry". Her coach went on to tell her how important it is for her to identify her emotions so that she can regulate her responses to others.

After the conversation with her former coach, Angie began to take more deliberate interest in her own self-awareness, and ultimately, she began to integrate strategies into her practices that helped her students build their personal self-awareness.

Based on what you have learned about *identifying emotions,* write a short email to Angie, from her former coach, that gives her some specific steps on identifying her own emotions, so that she might also help her ballet dancers develop self-awareness skills. Also, add a strategy that Angie might implement to help the dancers recognize their strengths and areas of growth.
See Appendix B - Strategies for Social-Emotional Growth.

Activity #4: Email Correspondence (Individual)

New Message

To: Angie
From: Angie's Former Coach
Subject: Helpful Tips

Send

Angie's Ballet All-Stars (Part 3)

At the regional competition, Angie's team placed 2nd and she was proud of each ballerina for their performance. She also felt that the communication with the team had gotten better after she implemented a few strategies that were recommended by her former coach. The first strategy involved her scheduling individual 15-minute meetings with each of the 12 dancers over the course of two weeks. She invited parents because she felt it was necessary for parents to be involved in the discussion on their child's progress. She had never done this before but quickly realized how much more she learned about her dancers in just the 15-minute conversation. With the parents present, they were able to confirm their child's strengths and weaknesses, confirm their status on the team in relation to their teammates, and discuss how much confidence they had in each of the major performance categories. As a result, Angie felt communication with the dancers got better and she no longer had to prompt them to start ankle strengthening exercises before practice. One parent said, "It felt great to know that you value our daughters outside of ballet. You helped us affirm and validate our child."

Activity #5: Reflection (Group or Individual)

How were your recommendations similar or different than Angie's?

STRENGTHS & WEAKNESSES

When we think about strengths we typically think about things we do well. We may have been told this by other people, or we may have determined this on our own. For the most part, we may have been told throughout our lives that there are certain things we are just good at, and other things we aren't so good at. For me, I have been told that one of my true strengths is my ability to bring positive energy into spaces that might be gloomy or sad. In these moments, I feel a sense of purpose because I love seeing other people happy. One of the confusions I have seen in defining strengths is that we typically always associate a strength with what we do well. Not to confuse you, but a real strength is more than just your ability to do something well. Here's an example:

> *My husband absolutely loved building computers and collecting computers parts. This was around the time when we first got married.There were computer parts everywhere. In our garaage, in the converted attic space, I basically couldn't go into an area of our home where he spent time and didn't see some part to a computer. He was really good at building computers and he got so good at doing it, he eventually got into networking and went into a different direction in his career with this newfound knowledge and skills.*
>
> *This was fine and dandy until he started getting requests from friends and family members to fix their computers. He wasn't so excited in these moments and it actually made him experience a great deal of anxiety when he would get calls from people to "come check out" their computers. After a few years of working in a position that required him to work on computers daily, he decided that he could no longer spend his off time helping friends and family with their technical issues.*

So, what many might perceived as a strength of my husband was not a strength at all, it was actually a weakness and caused him anxiety. See, though he knew how to build and fix computers, the real strength was his ability to focus on an independent problem, explore several options to solve the problem, and work independently to solve it. I notice it when he works on projects around the house like building a shed, putting in a sprinkler system, installing a synthetic lawn, and doing masonry work around the flowerbed. After he realized this, he was able to articulate this strength better, and to this day, understanding this strength has really helped him grow in his career, business, and personal life.

Let me admit something here. When I mentioned I like to bring joy to people, I had been living the majority of my work life saying "I want to work with the elderly." I felt this would really bring me joy and I had an opportunity to do this a little over ten years ago. It started off as an exciting adventure, but it soon became extremely draining when the health of many residents declined quickly and I became an emotional wreck. After a few months, I decided to move on and try something different. But, what I found out about myself, is that I still loved bringing happiness to people and I have been fortunate to be able to do that in different ways such as getting involved in more community service projects, dedicating more of my free time in my church, and being the chapter (CAAC) chaplain of my sorority, Delta Sigma Theta Sorority, Inc. I realized I needed to dig more to find the "sweet spot" in discovering not only the "what" but also the "how".

Answer the reflection questions on the next page. After you complete the set of questions, we will move on to **Growth Mindset** and **Self-Efficacy**.

Activity #6: Reflection (Group or Individual)

1. Now that we have discussed what a strength is, what do you think would be a good follow-up question that Angie's coach can pose to Angie?

2. What are your personal strengths and weaknesses?

Strengths:

Weaknesses:

3. What strategies did Angie use to discuss strengths and weaknesses with her team?

4. What other strategies could Angie use to help her students become more aware of their strengths and weaknesses?

GROWTH MINDSET

Growth mindset is more than simply understanding and accepting the scientific evidence that brain density and neuron expansion can lead to increased function, it is more about embracing the idea that intelligence is not fixed. According to Carol Dweck (2008), learners with fixed-mindsets are concerned more about external rewards and those with growth-mindsets focus on learning. Learners with fixed-mindsets believe that a great majority of intelligence is acquired at birth and this creates lifelong advantages over those who are not gifted with innate cognitive advantages.

One factor that contributes to outcomes that is oftentimes overlooked is motivation. Essentially, motivation explains why a person chooses to do a particular thing. Empirical studies have proven that intrinsic motivational orientations are critical components to the creative process. Those who are intrinsically motivated to engage in a particular activity are far more likely to undertake that activity voluntarily, and learn regardless of how challenging the activity. Whereas external controls such as grades, certificates, and other accolades are considered extrinsic motivators, those who are intrinsically motivated are moved by the challenge and curiosity of the activity itself.

Carol Dweck coined the term **growth-mindset** and offers two frames of thinking when dealing with the mental state of individuals as they approach a challenge. On one hand, those who are fixed in their ways find it difficult to adapt to the dynamic nature of problems that require new reasoning and a fresh way of approaching these problems. While those who possess a fixed mindset rely on their current knowledge and understanding, those with a growth-mindset see obstacles and challenges as building blocks along the journey to success.

Mindset permeates every aspect of one's life and has a huge impact of the type of life a person experiences. In *Mindset: The New Psychology of Success*, Dweck takes a glimpse of various fields and occupations such as teachers, coaches, athletes, and business leaders and give specific examples on how having a positive outlook and growth mindset can change outcomes. She shares how Jack Welch, former CEO of GE took over in the early 1980's and turned the company around and made it one of the most profitable corporations on the planet. He focused on teamwork, valuing employees, accepting challenges, and learning to foster growth in his employees through mentoring. This helped him to be one of the greatest business minds of our time and is an example of how having a growth mindset can change a corporate culture. Any adult working with youth is in a similar position to change how youth view struggle. Based on Dweck's study, learners with fixed-mindsets sometimes view themselves as "stupid" when they fail and oftentimes blame it on teachers, coaches, mentor, etc. She believes that adults can change this by shifting a childs' thinking of struggle and challenge from failure to opportunities for growth. This leads us to self-efficacy.

SELF-EFFICACY

I *(DuBois McMillan)* conducted a research study on the self-efficacy levels of six middle school-age youth from Los Angeles in the YMA program. Self-efficacy is a strong predictor of students' academic and social-emotional intelligence that influence life trajectories (McMillan, 2018). I made the theoretical proposition that embedding efficacy-building strategies into instruction would increase learners' self-efficacy levels. According to Bandura (1994), self-efficacy is one's belief in their ability to perform at designated levels regardless of obstacles that may impede them. Self-efficacy is an important element of intrinsic motivation (*motivation from within*) and plays a critical role in one's belief about their capabilities.

Whereas self-esteem is about how one feels about their self-worth, self-efficacy deals specifically with self-judgment of capabilities. Here's an example. I know how to drive a manual shift car. My brother taught me how to drive his Porche 914 when I was 14 years-old. That has been several decades ago, and I'm still quite confident that I can still drive a manual shift car. I have a high level of self-efficacy towards driving a car with a manual transmission and no one call tell me I can't because I know I can do it. That's what we call a high level of self-efficacy towards a particular function. Now, let's take a look back at Bandura's definition: *one's belief in their ability to perform at designated levels regardless of obstacles that may impede them.* In my opinion, the importance of self-efficacty lies in one's ability to push through setbacks and view these obstacles as opportunities to learn. So, if I get back into a manual shift car, believing I can drive one, and perhaps things don't go quite well and I shift too early, too late, or even grind on the clutch, I won't view these as "failed" attempts, I would view them as indicators that I just need to get use to shifting again. Here, I'm confident in my capabilities even though I'm not performing at my expected level quite yet. So, you might ask, "Where does self-efficacy come from?"

In Bandura seminal work, *Self-Efficacy: The Exercise of Control,* he outlines four ways in which to build self-efficacy. He believed these are antecedents (*comes before*) to building self-efficacy and there is a huge body of work by other researchers that support this idea. Here they are:

- **Mastery Experiences:** personal experieces where one masters a paticular thing;
- **Vicarious Experiences:** witnessing others similar to you successfully master a particular task;
- **Verbal Persuasion:** having someone giving positive verbal feedback and encouragement you while you are completing the task;
- **Physiological State:** being in a positive emotional state has an affect on how you approach a task (Bandura, 1994).

High-levels of self-efficacy have been linked to increased motivation, personal well-being, and personal achievement. Think about specific functioning domains where you feel extremely confident. It could be something as simple as throwing a ball, sewing, planting a flower, etc. Chances are, you have gone through one or several of the processes above.

Activity #7: Reflection (Group or Individual)

List two things that you feel high levels of self-efficacy for?

Activity #8: Growth Mindset and Self-Efficacy (Group or Individual)

Complete the Venn Diagram below by listing similarities and differences between Growth Mindset and Self-Efficacy.

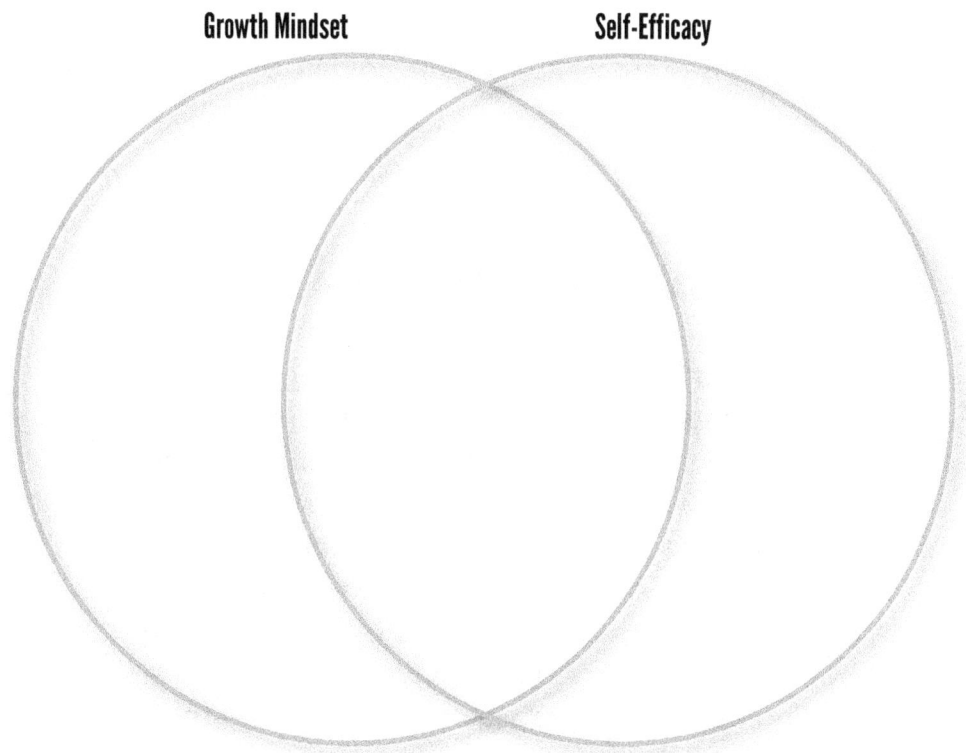

CHAPTER 2 PROJECT: HELPING ANGIE

Like many other adults who work with children, we cannot stress enough the importance of clear and transparent communication. This will increase the chances of building strong relationships built on sound principles. There will be times when messages are misinterpreted and this might cause some level of confusion. If our goal is to create spaces and communities that are healthy and supportive, then we must be able to think about how we create and shape these communities. Read *Angie's Ballet All-Stars Part 4* below:

Angie's Ballet All-Stars Part 4

After placing 2nd in the regional competition, Angie felt good that she had started to build rapport with her team. She even decided to have a small social gathering at a local park to get them to engage outside of the studio. This is what her former coach advised and Angie believed it really helped the team bond. But, she couldn't quite get one thing out of her mind that was said in one of the interviews by one of the dancers. The dancer said, "Angie never tells me I'm doing well or encourages me. She only says things when I do something wrong."

Angie wanted to address this statement, but thought she would wait until the season was over. She didn't want to spoil the success that team was having, and she really didn't know how to address it at the time because according to Angie, "I encourage everyone."

If you are in a group setting, form a small group and discuss the TREC Method before completing the skit on the next page. The TREC Method is a great way to get your ideas on paper before using them in a scenario. Go through each line and answer each question. When you are finished, apply what you have learned throughout this chapter to the skit. You will be giving Angie guidance on how to address the issue presented in Part 4 of her dilemma. There is no right or wrong answers here. I only recommend that you use the TREC Method as a guide to create your response. You will be pretending to be Angie's former coach.

Write your responses directly into the dialogue bubbles. Each response should align with one of the four areas of the TREC Method.

Activity #5: Discuss the TREC Method

Using the TREC Method to address the dilemma
(Guiding Questions)

What should Angie be thinking about?

THINK:

How would you advise Angie to ensure she shows respect as she addresses the problem?

RESPECT:

How would you advise Angie to demonstrate empathy for others in this dilemma?

EMPATHY:

What are some ways in which you feel Angie might show compassion by helping the dancer?

COMPASSION:

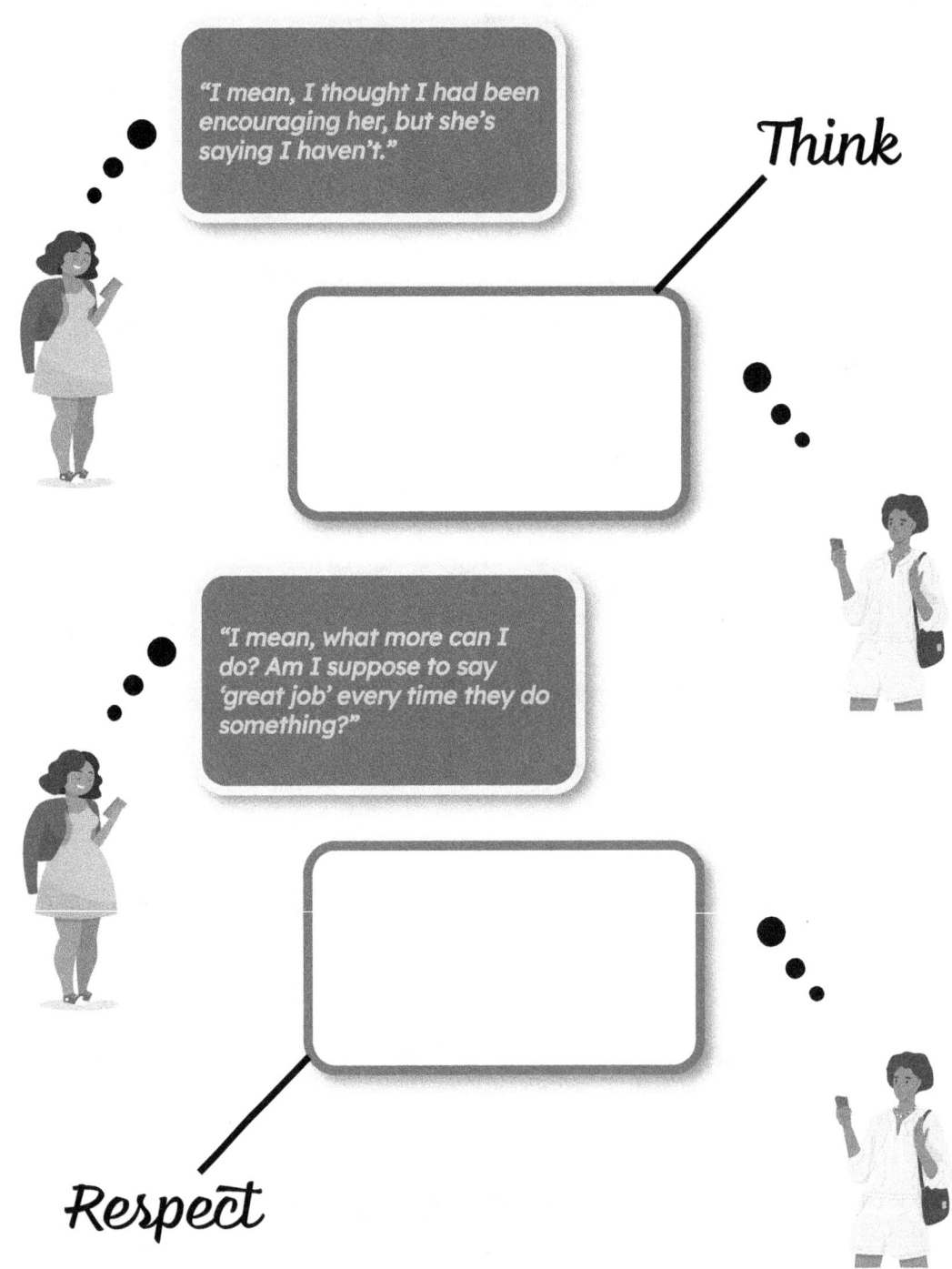

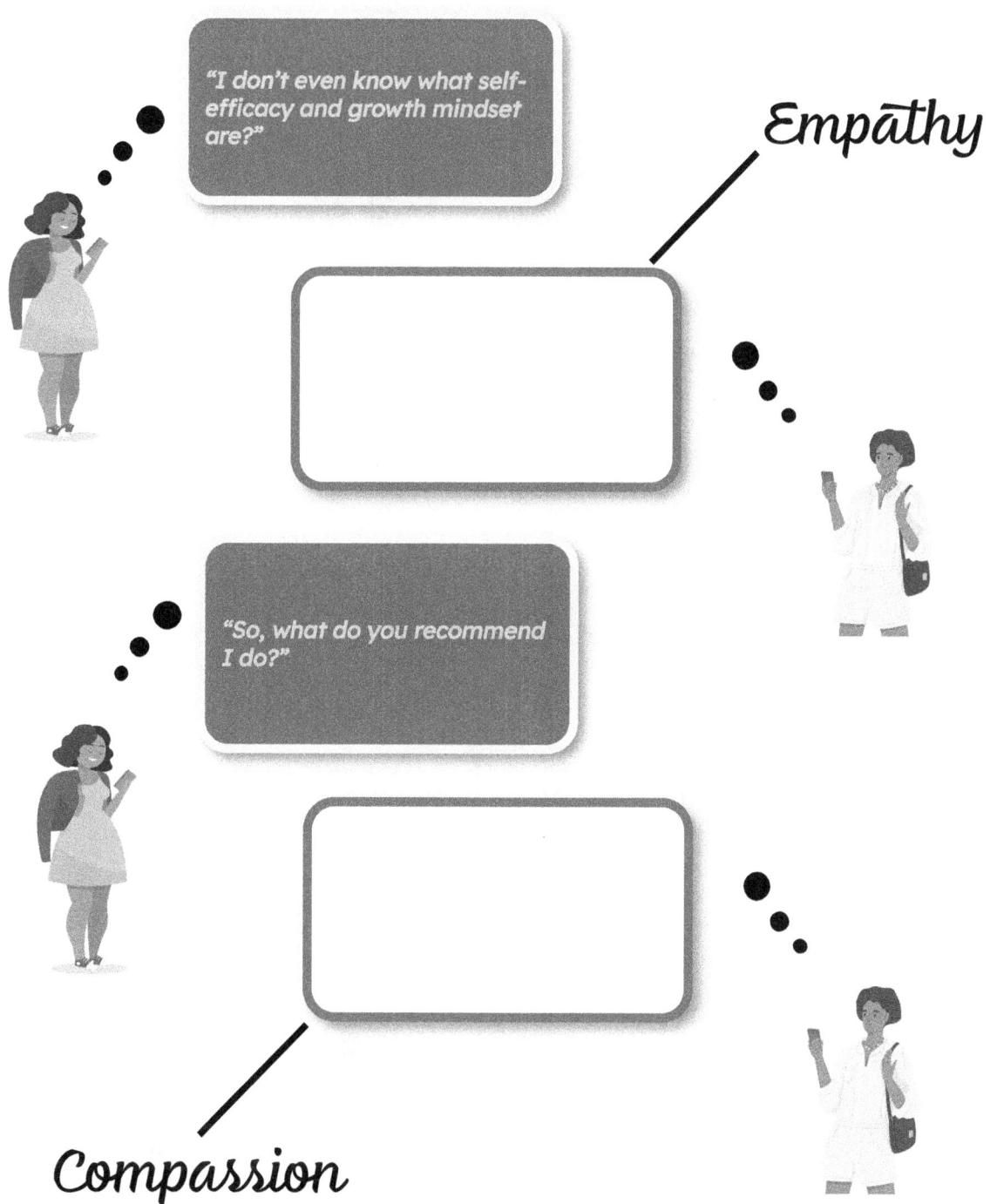

CHAPTER 2 CHECKUP

1. Self-efficacy is the same as self-esteem.

    True ☐ False ☐

2. Which of the following are components of **self-awareness** highlighted in the chapter?

    ☐ Growth mindset
    ☐ Identifying emotions
    ☐ Self-efficacy
    ☐ Self-reliance
    ☐ Strengths and weaknesses

3. Learners with fixed mindsets believe that a great majority of intelligence is acquired at birth and this creates life-long advantages.

    True ☐ False ☐

4. It is important to identify and control our emotions because this can help us regulate behavior and minimize _____ .

5. Which of the following are specifics examples of growth mindset that we might see in our every day lives:

    ☐ "Science is a challenge for me, but with practice I will improve."
    ☐ "I'll never learn how to program a computer. It's too hard for me."
    ☐ "When I receive constructive feedback, it helps me learn and grow."
    ☐ "What did I do wrong? I want to know so that I can do better."

CHAPTER 2 REFLECTION ACTIVITY FOR ECE EDUCATORS

Challenge your understanding of the Self-Awareness competency. The following vignette describes a preschooler who needs help engaging with his peers and managing his emotions.

It's a hot day outside in sunny California. Ms. Tee has activities set up in her shaded back yard for her daycare children. Their ages range from 18 months to 4 years old. Joshua, a strong-willed 4 year-old, has been with Ms. Tee since he was an infant and she knows him well. Since this is the only daycare Joshua has ever attended, Joshua has a hard time when new kids enroll in the daycare. Joshua has difficulty accepting and owning behaviors when he is wrong.

Joshua and Nik are playing at the water and sand table and Joshua takes a plastic shovel away from Nik. Nik begins to cry, and Joshua denies that he did it. When Nik walks over to tell Ms. Tee what happened Joshua throws one of the other play tools in the direction of Nik.

What is Joshua experiencing?

What can Ms. Tee do to help Joshua label and manage his emotions?

*Please see Appendix B for tips on strategies for the Self-Awareness competency

Chapter 3
Self-Management
When we are able to manage ourselves better, we are better people.

The purpose of this chapter is to explore self-management so that we can understand ourselves better, assist children in identifying stressors, and be able to interact with others in more constructive and positive ways.

...what you will be able to do at the end of this chapter:

- understand how to regulate one's emotions, thoughts, and behaviors in various scenarios.
- manage stressful situations better by using impulse control techniques.
- set personal goals and create a plan to achieve these goals.

...materials needed for this chapter:

- no additional materials are needed for this chapter.

Controlling our thoughts, speech, and behaviors are critical to building healthy relationships.

Self-Management (An Introduction)

Self-management is about being able to control your thoughts, emotions, and behaviors, and also being able to plan and prioritize your activities in order to achieve goals. We will explore several components of Self-Management (impulse control, stress management, self-discipline, self-motivation, goal setting, and organizational skills) and discuss ways that self-regulation can lead to positive interactions with others and also help us acheive goals.

In this chapter, you will explore self-management through dialogue with others, short vignettes, and a scenario-based activity where you will make decisions on how to respond in a lifelike situation.

At the end of the chapter, you will be more aware of how self-management can help control and manage thoughts and behaviors, and ways to plan and prioritize activities so that you can help children accomplish goals at a high level.

Knowing Her Students

Miss Stallings was a first-year teacher and was having trouble controlling her math class. Timothy had a tendency to blurt out answers without raising his hand and this totally disrupted learning in the classroom. Miss Stallings spoke to the counselor and he suggested that she created an agreement with Timothy. She and Timothy developed a system where he would tape a piece of masking tape to the top edge of his desk, and when he got the urge to blurt out answers before being called on, he would glance at the tape as a reminder for him to raise his hand. Whenever he controlled his impulse to blurt out the answers and raised his hand, Miss Stallings gave him a bonus ticket that he could use towards purchasing snacks from the student store.

Activity #1: Miss Stallings and Timothy

1. What can you say about the relationship between the teacher and the student?

2. What steps do you think Miss Stallings took to get to this point?

3. How do you think the use of this strategy has affected their relationship?

What is Self-Management?

When the concept of self-management is broadly analyzed in view of a child, we say that it is created on a baseline of self-awareness. Therefore, a child who has acquired self-management skills can identify their feelings, understand how these feelings affect their behavior, and learn to act better and more appropriately on those feelings.

Nevertheless, self-management is a little more than actions based on feelings. To fully understand its meaning, we must look at a broader perspective. In the social and emotional learning (SEL) context, self-management is about regulating one's thoughts, behaviors, and emotions effectively in diverse or unexpected situations (CASEL, 2017). More and more people who work with children are beginning to understand that in order to attain academic, personal, or group success, positive social behaviors and peer interactions are critical. Therefore, when kids learn to manage stress, motivate themselves, control impulses and work towards achieving their goals, whether these goals are academic, individual or group, they have a much better chance of achieving success when they are able to regulate their own behaviors (Malone, 2019). There is an obvious need for us to explore self-management so that we can help children, and perhaps ourselves, acquire these skills.

> "More and more people who work with children are beginning to understand that in order to attain academic, personal, or group success, positive social behaviors and peer interactions are critical."

Self-management is an essential concept because kids have different demands on their time and attention, from distractions in the family to distractions at school, from peers, and everything in between. When children understand themselves better, they are in a better place to manage their priorities (Malone, 2019). Overall, the goal of self-management is to teach kids the value of independence and self-reliance. However, research has equally shown that self-management strategies can be used to boost productivity, time-on-task, academic performance, and minimize problematic behaviors (Robbins et al., 2004). We will explore both aspects of self-management in order to help children meet the demands of our ever-changing world.

Becoming successful as kids is not about knowing more than others know. It is about being able to motivate ones self, assess and use knowledge and acquired skills, and change behaviors when it impairs learning (Kadiyono, 2017). According to Zimmerman and Martinez-Pons (1988), those with self-management skills know how to set goals, solve problems, and think positively no matter the kind of challenges, academic demands, and limitations of their environment. On the other hand, those lacking these skills may consider failure-avoiding strategies like copying from their peers, avoiding being called on in class, or appearing to work hard when in fact, they are doing the exact opposite (Kadiyono, 2017). When children have high self-management skills, research shows that they have greater resilience, capacity to adapt to change, self-reported well-being and higher academic performance (Agolla & Ongori, 2009). As we look back on Miss Stallings and Timothy, we see that she used a specific strategy to help Timothy develop valuable skills, but it also helped her control her classroom environment. So, we see the importance of self-management in how it helps individuals, but also how it extends to broader contexts.

Concerning the social and emotional learning context, kids must, therefore, develop skills and abilities in the following areas to develop their effective self-management skills:

- Impulse control
- Stress management
- Self-discipline
- Self-motivation
- Goal setting (CASEL, 2022)

Impulse Control

Impulse control, otherwise known as self-control or self-regulation, can be defined as the ability to alter or manage responses to improve desirable behaviors and avoid undesirable ones to accomplish long-term goals (Duckworth et al., 2016; Mofitt et al., 2011). When kids are not able to control their impulses, this might lead to behavior problems and cause others to be hurt or harmed, or processes disrupted in some way.

Several studies have shown that a high level of self-control gives rise to positive health and well-being (Shoda et al., 1990; Moffitt et al., 2011). According to Tangney et al. (2004), the extent of self-control has significant impacts on achieving higher grades and academic accomplishments, as well as better interpersonal relationships and happier lives (Hofmann et al., 2014; Vohs et al., 2011). Another study further shows that the lack of impulse control can become a barrier that keeps us from fulfilling our goals (Tangney et al., 2018). This study especially showed that the lack of self-control could hinder kids from getting higher test scores, and better grades in school.

Activity #2: Impulse Control Strategies

Below is a list of impulse control strategies. Read through the list and choose three strategies that you have used in the past. Discuss with a partner. As you are discussing, think of the following:

- Was this strategy effective?
- Why was it effective or not effective?
- How do you know it was effective or not effective?

Impulse Control Strategies

- Establishing rules
- Teach how to label feelings
- Problem-solving skills
- Create a reward system
- Teach anger management skills
- Respond to positive behaviors and negative behaviors equally
- Help child develop pre-planned responses to peer pressure
- Using a daily planner
- Play impulse control games

Others:

Stress Management

Monica has always loved computers. She started taking devices apart when she was only five years old to examine how all the parts are put together inside. She was mesmerized when she saw her first breadboard, with all of the wires neatly connected to it. She quickly learned about integrated circuits, resistors, and other parts inside of radios and other gadgets laying around the house. Her parents, seeing that she was interested in electronics, purchased her kits and she worked her way through each one of them rather quickly.

Now going into the 8th grade, she convinced her parents to sign her up for a local robotics team because she wanted to be prepared for the high school team and believed this would be a great opportunity for her.

After joining the team, Monica soon realized that robotics wasn't limited to the construction of hardware parts, she would have to learn how to program the robot, which was something she wasn't quite prepared to do. Her coach encouraged her to take home the programming sheet to study basic programming tasks, but it was difficult for her to grasp the concepts. After missing a few practices and ignoring her teammates text messages, she finally responded to her teammates with this message:

Activity #3: Stress Management

Monica was adamant about leaving the team. She had not spoken to her parents about leaving. She told them she was going to practice, but would actually spend time walking in the local park. Her teammates shared the news with the coach, who then called her parents and made them aware of what was going on.

1. Describe what you think Monica is feeling right now.

2. What concerns do you think her parents are having? How can they use TREC?

3. How should the coach handle this situation using the TREC Method?

Stress management refers to having the ability to control one's level of stress which leads to a more balanced and healthier life. We must recognize that stress is a part of our everyday activity, which makes controlling it really important. Living a happy and successful life begins with our ability to identify triggers that might cause stress and apply strategies to cope with it, but this is easier said than done.

Unfortunately, most adults recognize that stress is a part of their lives but fail to understand that children face stress as well. On many occasions, the sources of stress for children might be the same as adults, or it might come from unknown sources. From overpacked schedules to meeting the expectations of their friends and families, children deal with many stressors daily, which can inhibit development if not managed effectively..

> **"teach children how to combat stressors because most children may not understand that the feelings they have are stress, and it can make kids exhibit bad behaviors."**

Therefore, it is important to teach children how to combat stressors because most children may not understand that the feelings they have are stress, and it can make kids exhibit bad behaviors. According to a national survey by WebMD, over 72% of children exhibit negative behaviors as a direct result of stress (WebMD, 2017). Children can also show the following symptoms when stressed: headaches, stomach pains, mood swings, sleeping problems, difficulty concentrating in school, and changes in behavior.

Without stress management, children become overwhelmed, and many of them may not learn how to handle stressful situations and cope with problems. Therefore, teaching kids to cope with stressful situations can help them become more resilient and get through tough situations. **As we consider ways to assist Monica in this scenario, what are some things for us to consider? Write down two things below.**

One thing to consider is:

Another thing to consider is:

Strategies for Dealing with Stress

To manage stress, parents are encouraged to create a regular exercise plan for their children and enroll them in a recreational activity. A study showed that teaching children to engage in relaxation techniques such as mindfulness meditation and yoga could help them deal with stress and anxiety. This activity, especially, can help them handle stress and channel their emotions into improving their overall well-being. Children should be taught to prioritize, manage their time, and get adequate rest. These are basic things that we can do to help manage stress. As adults, we should also provide a stress-free environment for children by being positive, giving praise, teaching fairness, and showing them love and encouragement frequently (Allen, 1988). Being intentional is key. This might mean that we sit down with children and ask them about activities they enjoy and find opportunities in your local community for them to join. For instance, my son expressed that he liked skateboarding when he was in middle school. Well, we sat down, found skateboarding parks near our home, and I took him there often. He loved it so much that his aunt would also take him. Now that he's an adult, he keeps his skateboard in the trunk of his car and he still goes to the skate park a few times a week. He said the skate park is a "safe environment" and it helps him "relieve stress".

Self-Discipline

Self-discipline is about having the ability to resist distractions and temptations. It is also about not giving up, despite setbacks or failures.

Teaching kids about self-discipline is about teaching them to determine between positive and negative choices in order to make the right choices. A study by the American Psychology Association (2012) revealed that the lack of self-discipline could limit people from making healthy lifestyle decisions or improving their lives. Many other studies have equally shown that exhibiting a high level of self-discipline can boost academic performance (Anila, 2016; Duckworth & Seligman, 2005). Self-discipline can have a profound impact on one's life.

High levels of self-discipline can lead to stronger levels of confidence, and increases our ability to accomplish goals (De Ridder et al., 2012). When kids are taught to exhibit high levels of self-discipline, they can better control their routine activities, avoid problems, cope better with others, and overcome challenges (Hofmann et al., 2012). One of the best ways to teach self-discipline is by modeling the behavior. Here's an example:

Mr. Sampson was a second year math teacher. He had established great rapport with parents and students and was one of the most popular teachers on campus. One student posted this on the school's website:

> *"I just love Mr. Sampson's class. He goes over the work with us daily and he always has positive things to say to us."*

After receiving an email message from a parent complaining that Mr. Sampson didn't take out enough time with her child, Mr. Sampson became infuriated because he realized how much time he put into his job. This message caught him off guard, and as he pressed "reply" on the email message, he thought about all of the extra time he spent working with this particular student and felt unappreciated. He texted one of his colleagues and informed him that he would be late to the department meeting. "I'm about to give this parent a piece of my mind," he thought to himself.

Activity #4: Self-Discipline

1. What emotions do you think Mr. Sampson is feeling in this moment?

2. What advice would you give Mr. Sampson?

In this scenario, it's probably best that Mr. Sampson doesn't respond to the email in the moment. He is upset, emotionally charged, and might type a message that he will regret in the future. We chose to use an adult in this scenario because we understand the importance of adults having the self-discipline to control matters and not let things distract them from what they need to do. Because of this distraction, he is now late to an important meeting. We are not saying the email isn't important and he should not respond, what's important here is that he thinks about setting a better time to respond to the message when he's able to be thoughtful about what he writes.

When dealing with children, it's important that we teach them how to delay gratification in order to accomplish a short or long term goal. For instance, if a child has an important project to turn in that they haven't completed, but they want to go out with their friends the night before, how do we help them develop the skills to prioritize their tasks so that they can meet deadlines and also be able to engage in social activities with their friends?

Here's another example: What if two pre-schoolers are adamant about playing with the same toy? How might you deal with this dilemma?

Here are some skills that we can teach them:
- Problem-solving skills
- Organizational skills
- Goal setting
- Praising good behavior
- Give logical consequences for behaviors
- Model self-discipline yourself (CASEL, 2022)

Self-Motivation

Engaging students in problem-solving during math class often elicits collective groans from Mrs. Cary's 9th-grade Algebra I students. On multiple occasions, she had asked them why they disliked mathematics. Some students responded honestly and said "it's hard" or "it's stupid". Others talked about "how they will never use any of it in the real world" and believed it was a complete waste of time. This was disheartening for Mrs. Cary, she believed students should already know the importance of mathematics and didn't think it was her job to motivate students about something they should just normally want to learn. After talking to a colleague, she was told to try other methods to get students excited about learning math. Since Mrs. Cary does not have the extra time to adjust her pacing guide to include motivational strategies, she has observed a further decline in student interest, leading to her classroom average dropping to a "C-" by the end of the first semester.

Activity #5: Self-Motivation

1. What is the issue here?

2. What should Mrs. Cary do?

Regardless of how much we want our kids to succeed, success comes from the drive behind the actions we take. This drive or desire is called *motivation*. We can equally refer to self-motivation as having the self-perceived ability to complete a particular thing.

According to Neff (2015), we must teach kids to see the reasons why they must achieve the end goal and get them to embrace the learning process. According to this study, children are already aware of the consequences of failing, so self-motivation, primarily when fueled by self-compassion shifts your child's focus to help them take risks, experiment, try new things and keep moving on even in the presence of defeat (Neff, 2015).

It is equally important that we understand that no child is entirely unmotivated (Lynch, 1990). Therefore, when kids appear not to be motivated about schoolwork, it is usually because they are highly motivated by other activities (Lynch, 1990). These activities are usually things they are more "intrinsically" motivated to do. This means that they enjoy the activity itself and are more inclined to engage in it.

Goal-Setting

Goals refer to the valued outcomes we hope to accomplish when we carry out particular actions. Goals can also guide our activities, and we may orient our mind-set and environment in a manner that regulates behavior. Goal setting also provides a sense of purpose that gives us the drive to accomplish goals. Clear objectives provide clear and defined paths to success. Nevertheless, we must teach kids not just about setting goals, but creating goals that are meaningful. According to Srivastava (2009), all things being equal, we become more persistent in achieving a goal when we value the goal we set out to accomplish. When we encourage our kids to set and implement goals, we help improve their confidence, build their self-esteem, make better decisions, and help them remain focused. Naturally, children have the innate ability to set goals. However, they need encouragement to develop deeper goal-setting abilities (Saeed, 2012). When children are taught to set goals, it significantly increases the likelihood of boosting their self-confidence and self-efficacy.

Mr. Nelson is teaching his class about setting goals. However, he wants to go beyond sharing fictional stories and discussing goals. Mr. Nelson decided to use visual SMART Goal planners and worked with the children to come up with ideas for their personal and academic goals. He created charts illustrating the two types of goals, along with a separate chart for non-specific goals. Using a smaller planner, they organized these goals into smaller milestones. He also added a large star wall planner and awarded a star for each milestone completed, helping them focus on the individual steps toward their goals rather than solely on the outcome

At the end of each day, the kids discussed their efforts toward each goal and celebrated their accomplishments, no matter how small. He also provided individualized feedback on their progress, which appeared to boost students' excitement and confidence.

The key is teaching kids about goal setting and teaching them to make SMART (specific, measurable, attainable, relevant, and time-sensitive) goals (Doran, 1981). In addition, we must teach them to support these goals with a specific plan of action that fuels their drive to complete each step, which ultimately boosts success. We must also teach them to monitor and enjoy the process of achieving those goals. They must understand that the outcome is not nearly as important as the progress towards accomplishment. Nevertheless, we must also teach kids to celebrate the process of achieving those goals, no matter the outcome (Rijt et al., 2014). This means they must learn to acknowledge their own efforts positively and recognize areas for improvement (Dotson, 2015). This is another great example of self-awareness.

Organizational Skills

Many people have misconceptions about organizational skills. They believe that it is simply having the ability to keep things in order. However, organizational skills are more than remembering information or creating a list. It is about knowing how to handle information in a logical and effective manner. Having strong organizational skills is about being able to capture, process, organize, review, and carry out actions that lead to results.

When kids don't have great organizational skills, they may find it challenging making plans, setting priorities, staying on one task, or even accomplishing those tasks. Without strong organizational skills, it might be difficult for a child to organize their resources and thoughts in ways that will help them perform at optimal levels.

Sophie struggles to keep track of time when completing tasks at school. Ms. Emma is concerned about Sophie's organizational skills and often needs to prompt her during instructional time, which takes time away from other students. To address this, Ms. Emma and the school counselor developed a system to help Sophie monitor and manage her time. They provided a visual timer for the entire class and individual timesheets for Sophie and other students. These sheets included a chart of the day's tasks with columns for Sophie to record what she did and reflect on how she accomplished each task. At the end of the day, Sophie met with the teacher to review her timesheets and discuss her thought processes and daily achievements.

Organizational skills extend beyond the classroom. Possessing strong organizational skills can lead to significant accomplishments in various aspects of life. These skills are associated with higher productivity, better concentration, and improved memory.

CHAPTER 3 PROJECT: DEVELOPING A SMART GOAL

A S.M.A.R.T. goal is a goal that we set by using the a mnemonic acronym that stands for the following:

Specific: the goal should consist of a single thought or idea

Measurable: the goal should have objectives that you can track and measure

Actionable (Attainable): the goal should include clear tasks and actions

Realistic: the goal should be realistic for you to accomplish

Time: the goal should fall within a certain time frame

SMART goals are easy to write and they can really help you come up with a simple plan of action to successfully accomplish what you set out to do.

Here is a sample SMART goal. Let's say I want to write a business plan and it has five major parts to it. I've decided to give myself six months to write the plan and I will include several milestones along the way to ensure that I'm moving towards completing the plan by the end of the six-month period. You might be asking, "Why am I creating a SMART goal? Are we suppose to be helping children set goals?"

These are great questions! Later, you will help someone else write a SMART Goal.

SAMPLE SMART GOAL

Goal: To Write a Business Plan

By March 1, 2023 (TIME), I will complete a business plan (SPECIFIC). To complete this plan, I will write five sections that cover critical areas of the business (MEASURABLE-REALISTIC). I will write (ACTIONABLE) one part per month and check my plan monthly to ensure that I'm on course to complete the plan by the deadline (MEASURABLE).

Use the space below to write a simple SMART goal. As a guide, please insert the elements of a SMART Goal (specific, measurable, actionable, realistic, and time) like I did in the sample above.

WRITE A SMART GOAL

CHAPTER 3 CHECKUP

1. Self-management is about being able to control your emotions, thoughts, and behaviors.

   True ☐   False ☐

2. CASEL recommends that children develop skills and abilities in the following areas for effective self-management:
   - ☐ Self-motivation
   - ☐ Impulse control
   - ☐ Stress management
   - ☐ Self-discipline
   - ☐ Goal setting

3. Those with self-management skills know how to problem-solve, set goals, regulate behavior, and think positively when dealing with challenges.

   True ☐   False ☐

4. Self-discipline is about having the ability to resist distractions and temptations. It is also about not giving up, despite _____.

5. How does intrinsic motivation differ from extrinsic motivation? Use the space below for your response:

CHAPTER 3 REFLECTION ACTIVITY FOR ECE EDUCATORS

Challenge your understanding of the Self-Management competency. Please read the vignette and suggest what you would do in this scenario and how the teacher can apply the TREC Method in this scenario.

Ms. Karen's classroom, which she affectionately calls "The Park" operates like a well-oiled machine. She has been a lead Pre-K teacher for 3 years and takes prides in how well her students perform when they enter kindergarten. She is also extremely passionate about teaching and interacts well with her students. When evaluated Karen scores high in most of the areas around social-emotional and cognitive development. However, daily she is puzzled how she can better serve Blue. Blue is a 3-year-old from Haiti and he has difficulty dealing with disappointment and anger. Every day at the end of story time Ms. Karen prompts the children to begin singing the song to line up to go outside once their name is called. Blue never waits for his name to be called. Once the class starts singing Blue immediately jumps up and runs to the door to be first in line. Ms. Karen's assistant knows the routine and gently brings him back to sit on his circle to wait for his name to be called. She knows this causes him a high level of anxiety, so she sits next to him. However, it doesn't help on most days because he is already disappointed, and the anger has already set in. Blue begins kicking, screaming and sometimes he runs in circles in the classroom. These meltdowns last 5-10 minutes at a time and when its over he is embarrassed and has a hard time engaging in positive social peer interactions with his friends.

Briefly describe how you might use the TREC Method to address this issue?

Review Appendix B and list of strategy that you might use to help. Why would you use this strategy?

*Please see Appendix B for tips on strategies for the Self-Awareness

Chapter 4
Social Awareness

Our ability to understand others and have a sense of how they feel.

The purpose of this chapter is to understand how social awareness will help children build better relationships with others by learning the importance of empathy and respecting the feelings of others.

...what you will be able to do at the end of this chapter:

- define empathy.
- understand the difference between cognitive and emotional empathy.
- describe ways to demonstrate empathy in life-like situations.
- create a short script and role-play that demonstrates empathy.

...materials needed for this chapter:

- no additional materials are needed for this chapter.

You never know how someone else is feeling until you walk in their shoes.

Social Awareness: Introduction

Being aware is about having knowledge about something. It is about feeling, getting a sense of, perceiving, or being aware of events or situations. While self-awareness, which we have discussed previously, is about gaining that consciousness of ourselves, social awareness is about being conscious of others and things going on around you. Simply put, social-awareness is all about knowing about all of the things going on around you, particularly things going on with other people. In this chapter, you will explore social awareness through dialogue with others, short vignettes, and a scenario-based module where you will make decisions on how to respond in a lifelike situation.

At the end of the chapter, you will be more aware of its importance in helping children show empathy towards others with the goal of building better relationships. We will apply the TREC model to these scenarios.

Cathy's Story

Cathy was destined to be a teacher. Since her childhood, she always imagined herself in front of a class of excited and engaged learners. In her second year of teaching, she was known in her department as a teacher who really understands how to deliver purposeful lessons and master the timeline in her pacing guide. After introducing the upcoming unit at the end of class on the previous day, she was well prepared to open the lesson with a funny hook. While standing at her door and greeting her students before they entered the class, she overheard several students discussing a matter that was shown on the news the night before. One student was in tears and being consoled by her peers. It was obvious that the mood of the students was somber. Cathy was clearly aware of how events outside of her classroom could affect the classroom climate. In her lesson planning, she had embedded independent focus time to address unforeseen issues like this. She even developed a system where students could go to a cozy section of her room with a cushy chair at any point of feeling anxious, uneasiness, or just to relax and decompress.

Other background information:

- Cathy is falling behind in grading and must present at tomorrow's department meeting. Her goal is to get through the first lesson in the unit prior to the meeting
- The student who is crying has never shown this type of emotion in the past. So, Cathy doesn't have any additional background information on this matter

Activity #1: Cathy's Dilemma

1. What do you think Cathy should do first?

2. What is Cathy's dilemma?

3. What other ways can Cathy prepare for situations like this? What about other adults working with children?

In this scenario, Cathy makes two important **moves** that demonstrate her ability to handle unexpected moments when others need emotional support. Though these aren't the only ways that an informed and compassionate adult might respond, these steps are effective in meeting the social-emotional needs of the child. Here is the exhange between Cathy and the students:

> *During passing period, Cathy stood at her classroom door greeting students as they entered the classroom. She noticed two students walking with Elisa, who is visibly shaken and sobbing.*
>
> *"Good morning," Cathy said, as bubbly as she does daily. Karen and Bea had their arms around Elisa's shoulder as they entered the room, patting on her back, trying to console her as much as they could.*
>
> *"Good morning," Karen mumbled, Cathy stepped inside the door and watched the girls as they entered. She had never seen Elisa this emotional.*
>
> *"Elisa, are you okay? Cathy said, with a concerned look on her face. Elisa wiped her eyes, and nodded slightly. "Thank you so much Karen and Bea, you are fantastic. Thank you for helping Elisa to class." The class was nearly full by now and the chatter was rising in volume. "You have a moment to talk?" Cathy whispered to Elisa. Elisa nodded, and they walked to the safe place in the classroom.*
>
> *"I'm just so upset about what happened yesterday," Elisa said, releasing the pain that she has been trying to suppress.*
>
> *"I see. Yeah, it was painful to see. I'm even struggling with processing it, that's normal. But, would you like to talk a little later or would you like to talk to someone else now? I'm here for you and want to make sure you are okay."*
>
> *Elisa agreed to stay in class and discuss it later. Cathy reminded her of the classroom norm of going to the safe place at any point during class for a mental break. Elisa didn't use the safe place during class but did stay after class and a large portion of nutrition break sharing with her teacher, Cathy.*

4. Highlight or underline specific moves Cathy made in the scenario that demonstrate her use of the TREC (*think-respect-empathy-compassion*) Method in providing social-emotional support?

5. After reading through the scenario and analyzing some of the specific moves made by the teacher, complete the **Sentence Stems** below:

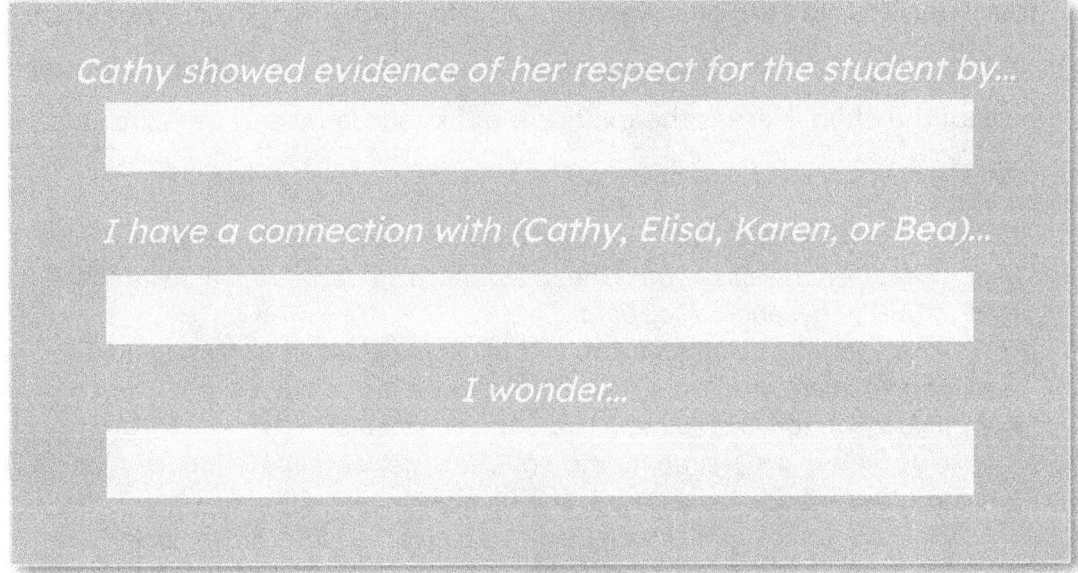

Cathy showed evidence of her respect for the student by...

I have a connection with (Cathy, Elisa, Karen, or Bea)...

I wonder...

6. Connect with a partner and discuss your responses to **Questions #4 and #5**. Read through each of the questions, then rotate.

1. Discuss one of the moves the teacher made.

2. How did Cathy demonstrate that she used the TREC method?

3. Which character did you connect with? In what ways?

4. What are you wondering?

The Importance of Social Awareness

In basic terms, **social awareness is the ability to get a sense of the emotional state of people around you, and being able to interact with them in appropriate ways.** Overall, it is about having an in-depth understanding of societal norms for behavior, struggles, cultures, problems, environment, and communal set-ups, so you can understand and respond effectively to the needs of others. On a much broader scope, social awareness is about making contributions to the nation, environment, and community. Hence, social awareness is about an individual's understanding of their social environment and how to respond to particular things that happen in these various spaces.

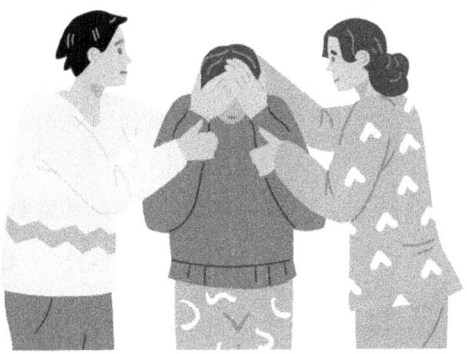

Despite their age and growing cognitive development, children often can discern the emotions of others from their non-verbal messages. They do this by observing the voice, tone, language, body language, and facial expression of others. They also often have a fantastic ability to relate with others, especially when their peers are bullied or hurt. Even infants typically attune themselves to other infant's feelings. This almost-supernatural connection between kids is the reason why we often see an infant cry when they hear another infant crying.

Furthermore, kids typically learn about the social world from their classmates, playmates, and family, which is quite different from adults, who can learn from the media, news, social media platforms, neighbors, friends, etc. This pattern of learning helps children to have a broader understanding of the world, and at this stage, they are also developing the ability to understand their feelings. As you might have imagined in Cathy's story, anyone coming in contact with children daily must be able to assess the emotional state of students continuously in order to meet their needs. This isn't limited to teachers. Coaches, recreational workers, social workers, neighbors, friends, family members -- we all need to know how to detect when someone is in need of support.

> **"It's up to us, as caring adults, to learn how to detect behaviors that might be detrimental to the emotional state of others."**

It's up to us, as caring adults, to learn how to detect behaviors that might be detrimental to the emotional state of others. We must help others navigate in our social world so that they are able to sense when they are experiencing periods of emotional distress, anxiety, depression, or other emotional challenges. Social awareness can help our kids become aware of how they fit into the world, as they develop values and attitudes about other people. By extension, social awareness can help kids understand the various social settings, and recognize class and race concerns in diverse circumstances, understand power dynamics and even create inclusive environments that respect and embrace differences.

SOCIAL AWARENESS IN THE CLASSROOM

When kids and adults have a strong social awareness in the many social settings where we might come in contact (school, playground, event, store, museum, sporting event, etc.), we can take our knowledge and skills on how to assess others into these spaces. This ease of adaptation happens when teachers, counselors, administrators, aides, custodians, coaches, specialists, students, and other staff members, can all relate with other's perspectives and be aware of how to assess behaviors that might be indicators of emotional challenges that children or adults might be facing. Therefore, when all the kids and adults in a particular class have strong social awareness, it can foster an environment where those kids can focus on learning, and have supports in place that foster an environment of support.

For adults working with children, it's important to build rapport with children and create opportunities for them to engage in cooperative work with their peers, build norms, implement strategies for team building, and other activities such gallery walks and peer sharing that encourages positive interactions.

Ideally, these opportunities will create a community of support where each child feels valued and appreciated, and in the event of a child showing signs of emotional distress or abnormal behavior, the chances of a community member detecting these moments is much greater.

SOCIAL AWARENESS IN BUILDING RELATIONSHIPS

Strong social awareness is prerequisite to better relationships. When we have strong social awareness, we can understand and communicate with others in a much better way. That way, we can feel what they are feeling and say the right words that are relevant to the situation. We can engage in constructive conversations with our peers and can resolve conflicts effectively. With this, kids can be open to learning from their peers and other social supports, which is a vital life skill. Therefore, social awareness influences social behaviors positively, and by so doing helps us establish and maintain relationships.

List 3 Benefits of Social Awareness

Elements of Social Awareness

By now you should have a good understanding on what social awareness is. In this section, we will take a closer look at the four areas of focus in social awareness. These areas are: perspective-taking, empathy, appreciating diversity, and respect for others.

PERSPECTIVE-TAKING

Perspective-taking is about being able to understand a concept or circumstance from an alternative view that isn't ours. When we can understand other people's perspectives, we can have great interactions with others. However, perspective-taking isn't all about discarding our own beliefs or judgment but letting the view of other people create a leeway for us to reassess our perspective to ensure that we consider the perspective of others.

Timothy is a successful tennis coach who has been running a successful youth program for eight years. He's ecstatic that his program has grown from only four players in its first year to now having over 40 kids in his program. He runs a strict program because he wants to prepare each of his players for high school and knows the demands can be hard on kids who are used to managing the rigors of school and playing sports. One rule he hasn't bended on in years is the club's dress code. His players must wear the appropriate tennis gear to practice, if not, they will get a warning the first time the rule is broken. On the second offense, there is a parent meeting and the player is liable to get released from the program.

Tasha is new to the program, but certainly not new to tennis. She is a stellar player who started swinging rackets when she was only four years old, and since then, her parents have had her in highly competitive tennis programs. Up until a few months ago, Tasha's life was going quite smoothly. She was doing well in school, having fun with her friends, and living the typical life of a thirteen year old kid. When her mother received an offer for a promotion that she had been waiting for, the family decided to take the leap and move to a new city. Her father and mother have always been supportive, so the first thing they explored was a local tennis club in the new city.

After budgeting the cost of living in a more expensive city, including the purchasing a new home and a newer car, they set a monthly budget for Tasha to join a well known tennis club that is assumingly best for her.

Joining the club was a breeze, and after only a few practices, Tasha is obviously one of the top performers in the entire club.

After the third practice, Timothy notices that Tasha is still wearing gear from her old club. He knows she has the gear, she wore it to the first practice. Timothy isn't upset that it's a team that his club has competed against in regional tournaments, he's more concerned that she's simply not wearing the club's practice gear. Timothy thought to himself, "I'm sure they got the message that she has to wear our gear. I was clear in the orientation meeting that she must wear our gear to every practive. She hasn't wore the right gear to two consecutives practices."

Activity #2: Tim's Tennis Club

1. What is Timothy's dilemma?

2. What are two things Timothy needs to consider as he *thinks* about his approach?

3. What should be Timothy's first course of action?

Use the TREC Method to address the dilemma

What should Timothy be thinking about?

THINK:

How can Timothy ensured he shows respect as he tries to address the problem?

RESPECT:

How can Timothy demonstrate empathy for Tasha and her family?

EMPATHY:

What are some ways in which Timothy might show compassion?

COMPASSION:

Other background information:

- Tasha's parents accidently purchased a gas dryer, not realizing that their new house has an electric hookup. Consequently, her uniform hasn't been washed
- With this new information, Timothy feels more comfortable approaching the family

In review, perspective-taking is being able to take an alternative view from your normal view or perspective on a situation. Having new information, how might your approach be different from your original approach? If your approach doesn't change in any of the areas, simply write "same" in the space. This scenario reminds us of the importance of "thinking" before we act.

Use the TREC Method to address the dilemma

What should Timothy be thinking about?

THINK:

How can Timothy ensured he shows respect as he tries to address the problem?

RESPECT:

How can Timothy demonstrate empathy for Tasha and her family?

EMPATHY:

What are some ways in which Timothy might show compassion?

COMPASSION:

EMPATHY

Empathy is about understanding another person's needs, concerns, and emotions. In a basic sense, it is about being able to understand what another person is actually experiencing. When we can respond to the feelings and needs of others, we encourage trust, which helps us to build strong relationships with others. Since you are already familiar with the TREC Method and have been working through scenarios and applying it in various contexts, you understand how important empathy is in making strong connections with others. These connections can directly affect one's situation and help them shift to a better place to be able to show their resilience in a tough situation.

Empathy typically falls into two major categories, and it's important that we explore both so that we can apply them in scenarios in this book, and begin thinking how we can apply them in real contexts that you might encounter in your life. Social emotional health is important, and one of the most powerful ways to support others is by showing empathy. Here are the two major forms of empathy:

- Feeling the same emotions as the next person (**emotional empathy**)
- Being able to reason from the perspective of others (**cognitive empathy**)

Emotional Empathy

With emotional empathy, we connect with someone else and a "shared experience" is created. We feel the same pain and begin to express compassion, or a willingness to help the person.

Cognitive Empathy

When we practice cognitive empathy, we are essentially taking the perspective of another person by trying to place ourselves in their situation in order to understand what they are feeling.

So, as we can see, empathy plays a major role in helping others when they are struggling with difficult challenges in life. The results from the California Healthy Kids Survey, show that there's a need for more social emotional support from caring adults and also a need for more awareness around harassment and bullying types of behaviors occuring at schools in California. The data from 2015-2017, show that 1 in every 3 students in the 7th grade expressed that they had been harassed or bullied within the last 12 months. Additionally, only 57% of all 9th graders and 61% of all 11th graders said they established caring relationships with adults at school.

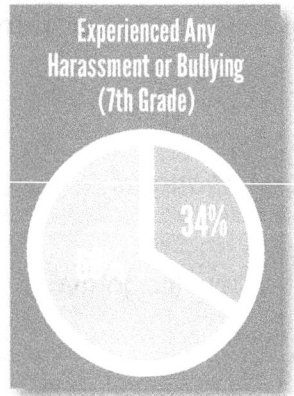
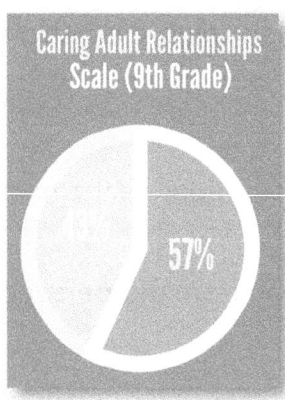
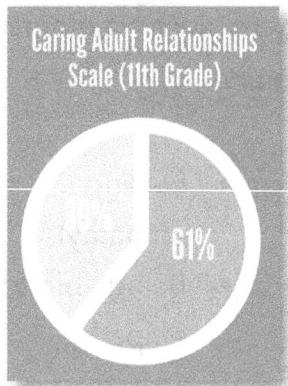

Source: California Health Kids Survey (2015-2017)

After viewing the data, what are you wondering?

Activity #3: Emotional Empathy versus Cognitive Empathy

Complete the Venn graph below by listing similarities and differences about emotional empathy and cognitive empathy. List similarities where the circles overlap.

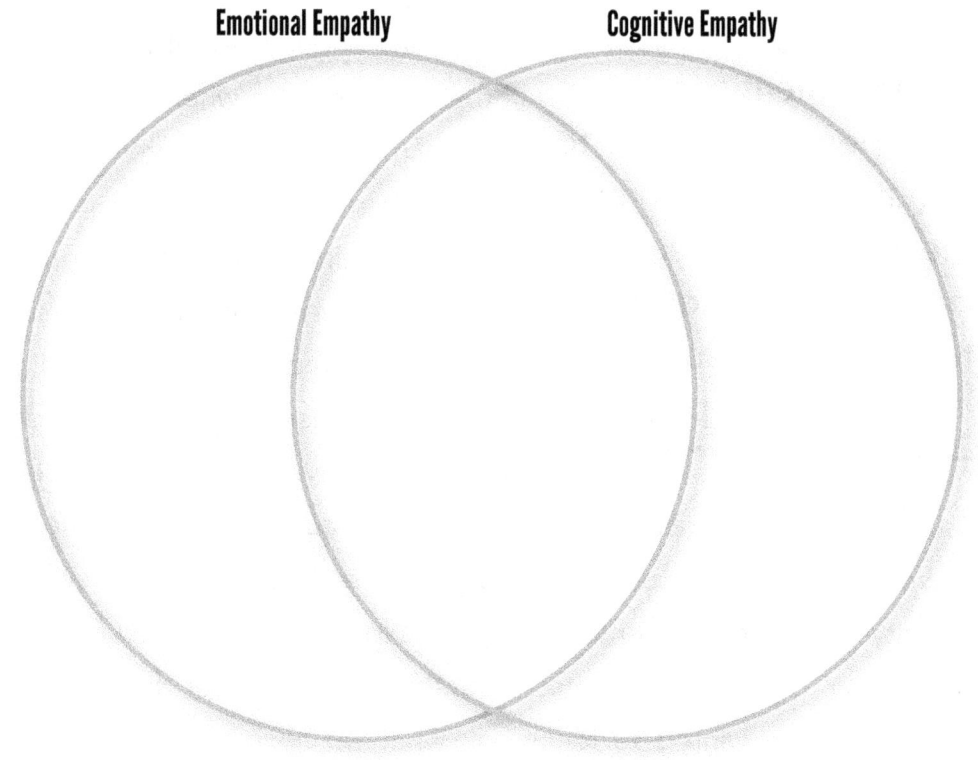

APPRECIATING DIVERSITY

I (DuBois) had a unique experience as an educator and school administrator. I was fortunate enough to work for a school district that happened to be the 4th most diverse school district in the nation. We oftentimes talk about diversity and inclusion, but when we think about how diversity actually plays out in a school setting, where students from various ethnic groups, socio-economic positions, different religious affiliations, races, are all grouped together in a single school commununity, there are many things to consider to ensure every student feels recognized, embraced, and supported. When we talk about appreciating diversity, one of the keys here is to think about how diversity makes us stronger as a human race.

"when we are intentional about bringing people together to share what we have in common, in some strange way, we learn about our own uniqueness and this makes us stronger as people."

I can't say enough about how amazing the experience was where I spent eight years of my professional career. As I think about diversity, there is one particular event that sticks out in my mind about the school community that I will share. There was a moment in my third year as an administrator where students decided to have an inter-cultural event opposed to a multi-cultural assembly. While some students opposed the idea, and to be honest, I wasn't sure if it was a good idea because to take away the opportunity for under-represented groups to express their cultural uniqueness in their school community seemed counterproductive, but students were adamant that they wanted to focus on "what we have in common". With the guidance of their amazing advisor, students had constructive discussions on the pros and cons of doing the event. Now, to give some context to the experience, the school community had various systems in place for students to express their voices, there were over 100 student-run clubs on campus, a vast number of athletic programs, community and parent involvement were high, and the school had earned the *Democracy School* designation. In a short conversation with one of the students who was on the planning committee for the event, she simply said, "learning about what we have in common made me feel even better about who I am."

My point for sharing this is to inform others of the value we gain when we are intentional about bringing people together to share what we have in common, and in some strange way, we learn about our own uniqueness and this makes us stronger as people.

Activity #4: Appreciating Diversity (Pair-Share)

In groups of two, answer these questions:

1. Is it important to appreciate what makes another person unique? Why?

2. How do respect and communication relate to appreciating differences?

3. What would be your biggest concerns related to diversity?

4. What is one characteristic about you that resonates most with others?

RESPECT FOR OTHERS

We have covered a lot on social awareness so far in this chapter. We took a look at perspective-taking and empathy, and applied the TREC Method to a scenario and also learned about two major forms of empathy (cognitive and emotional). We then discussed how appreciating and embracing differences make us stronger as a whole. To conclude this section, we will cover one of the most important topics that must be considered when discussing how we relate with others, and that's **respect.**

When we think about the basic definition of respect, we might come up with something along the lines of "having tolerance and accepting others as they are". With a quick search on the Internet, I find a more detailed meaning of the word. To be honest, it's a little surprising that Google is telling me respect is "a feeling of deep admiration for someone or something elicited by their abilities, qualities, or achievements". Okay, I get it. This type of repect is more about someone admiring another person because of some accomplishment. But, the type of respect I want to cover in this section is the type where everyone, regardless of their personal or group's accomplishments, is deserving of respect simply because they are another human being.

As we have been covering respect in the TREC Method, we understand the importance of recognizing someone else's feelings, emotions, and their humanity. This is important in establishing good rapport amongst children, and also between adults and children, whether it be at home, school, or other settings.

Activity #5: Definition of Respect (Pair-Share)

What is your definition of respect?

Is your definition similar to your partner's definition?

In a report by the Collaborative for Academic, Social, and Emotional Learning (CASEL, 2022), students in schools with a strong focus on social-emotional learning overwhelmingly reported having more positive experiences in school and feeling more respected by others. In this same report, there are some startling numbers regarding schools with strong SEL programs. In the findings, 9 out of 10 of the high schools surveyed believed their teachers and principals were supportive and respectful, compared to only about 50% of the students from schools who did not have strong SEL programs. The message is clear, students at schools with strong SEL programs feel respected by the adults they interact with in the school setting. When we compared this to only 61% of the students in *California Healthy Kids Survey* claim to having a caring relationship with an adult, the message is clear: *there is work to be done.*

CHAPTER 4 PROJECT: DIALOGUE TREE

In the space below, you will complete each of the dialogue branches to complete the tree. You recently heard that someone has been bullying Toya on social media. You see her near her locker and she looks really sad. What would you do?

CHAPTER 4 CHECKUP

1. When perspective-taking, it's important that you don't allow yourself to see the perspective of others.   True ☐   False ☐

2. Which of the following are components of Social Awareness?
    - ☐ Respect
    - ☐ Obedience
    - ☐ Perspective-taking
    - ☐ Empathy
    - ☐ Appreciating diversity

3. Cognitive empathy is when you take on the same emotion as another person.

    True ☐   False ☐

4. Students who attend school with strong SEL programs report that teachers and adults are _____ and _____.

5. How do respect and communication relate to appreciating differences? See **Appreciating Diversity** section from this chapter. Extend your response here.

CHAPTER 4 REFLECTION ACTIVITY FOR ECE EDUCATORS

Challenge your understanding of the Social-Awareness competency. Please read the vignette and answer the reflection questions at the bottom of the page.

Gabrielle is a 2-year-old girl who loves going to school. Most of the time, she enjoys playing alone. During outside time you will find her on the climbing apparatus, playing alone at the sand and water table, or riding the bike. Gabrielle's teacher is concerned that she chooses to be alone during her time at school. He encourages her to play with other children and he also creates opportunities for her to pair up with other students. Gabrielle will participate and engage and ask him often "When are we going outside"? Mr. Kevin shared his concern with Gabrielle's mother. Her mother explained that they live in an apartment and she doesn't have a bike or any space to play outside. So, when she is outside at school, she is exploring all the things she is unable to partake in at home.

How do you recommend her teacher move forward with this new information?

Review Appendix B and list a strategy that you might use to help. Why would you use this strategy?

*Please see Appendix B for tips on strategies for the Social-Awareness competency

Chapter 5
Relationship Skills

Building healthy relationships with others is an important part of life.

The purpose of this chapter is to help learners understand the importance of building healthy relationships with others from similar and diverse backgrounds.

...what you will be able to do at the end of this chapter:

- understand the importance of building relationship skills.
- apply strategies that can help improve relationships.
- use the TREC Method to navigate a scenario centered on resolving conflict.
- create a short script and role-play to address interpersonal conflict.

...materials needed for this chapter:

- no additional materials are needed for this chapter.

At the center of any healthy relationship lies one of life's greatest gifts: Respect.

Introduction: Relationship Skills

Since we were children, we have had to interact with others and build relationships. Some of these relationships may have been closer than others, like those with family members or close friends, or perhaps classmates, neighbors, coaches, or teachers. No matter how you came to develop these relationships with others, it's important to know that relationship skills are important to one's social-emotional health. In the last chapter, we focused a lot on looking at the emotional state of others and discussed ways to embrace diversity, and show empathy and compassion. In this chapter, we will shift and look at ways to build strong relationships with others and think of ways to resolve conflict.

By the end of the chapter, you will have a greater understanding of how to develop relationship skills and build stronger connections with others. Additionally, we will apply the TREC Method to two scenarios.

The Pianist (Part 1)

Linda is an aspiring pianist who has been training since she was five years old. She is now 16 and a junior in high school in an average size high school. In a recent meeting with her counselor, she was advised to join a student club or get involved in community service projects so that she can learn team-building and build relationships with others. This is a struggle for Linda, who spends much of her time away from the school mainly practicing on her grand piano in the living room of her home. Linda admits that she's an introvert and doesn't feel like spending her free time pretending to be interested in joining clubs or volunteering on projects just to make friends. She told her mother,

"That's weird. Why would I want to work with people just so that I can put that on a college application?" Her mother didn't respond, feeling that the idea did feel kind of strange. Linda's mother scheduled a meeting with the counselor to discuss the matter in more detail.

During the meeting, the counselor expressed her concerns that Linda hasn't made many friends over her three years of high school and she had some concerns that Linda hadn't even made an attempt to meet other students and build positive relationships. "I mean, is she required to have friends in order to graduate?" her mother asked. "It seems quite ridiculous to make my daughter make friends. The counselor felt her mother's resistance and felt she was becoming a bit contentious in her tone.

Other background information:

- **Linda's best friend moved during the first semester of their sophomore year and Linda hasn't seen her since she left. They communicate over social media every so often.**

- **Linda has never been part of a team or group. She self identifies as a loner and feels anxiety when she's in social settings.**

Activity #1: By Myself (Group or Individual)

1. What should the counselor do?

2. What are some additional questions you think the counselor might ask?

3. Do you support the graduation requirement? Why or why not?

4. What advice would you give the counselor? Linda's mother?

Relationship Skills

If we take a quick look at the student outcomes of any school across the country, we'll see that almost all schools will have a *Student Learning Outcome (SLOs)* or *Expected Schoolwide Learning Result (ESLR)* in some way connected with building strong relationships with others. Some states might simply call them goals, but in California, you are likely to see them as SLOs or ESLRs. Here is one that I randomly selected from a quick search on the Internet. I pulled this from a high school in Califronia:

> "Participate in group and class projects such as collaborative teams, peer editing, role-playing, speech presentations and/or video productions" (SAUSD, 2022).

Here is another one from a high school in Rancho Cordova, CA:

> "Responsible Citizens who:
> - Contribute time, energy, and talents to improve the welfare of themselves and that of others
> - Promote and model effective communication and respect among people of different lifestyles and cultures
> - Demonstrate habits of personal well-being and safety
> - Assume personal responsibility as a member of a family, a community and the world" (FCUSD, 2022).

As we can see, these goals extend beyond the individual and require learners to think about how they are connected with others and encouraged to work collaboratively. This is not limited to school systems, relationship skills are tranferrable across all industries and a requisite skill to be marketable in the diverse world we live in.

Activity #2: Student Outcomes - Internet Search (Group or Individual)

Conduct an Internet search and find learning outcomes from two organizations around communication, relationship building, or teamwork.

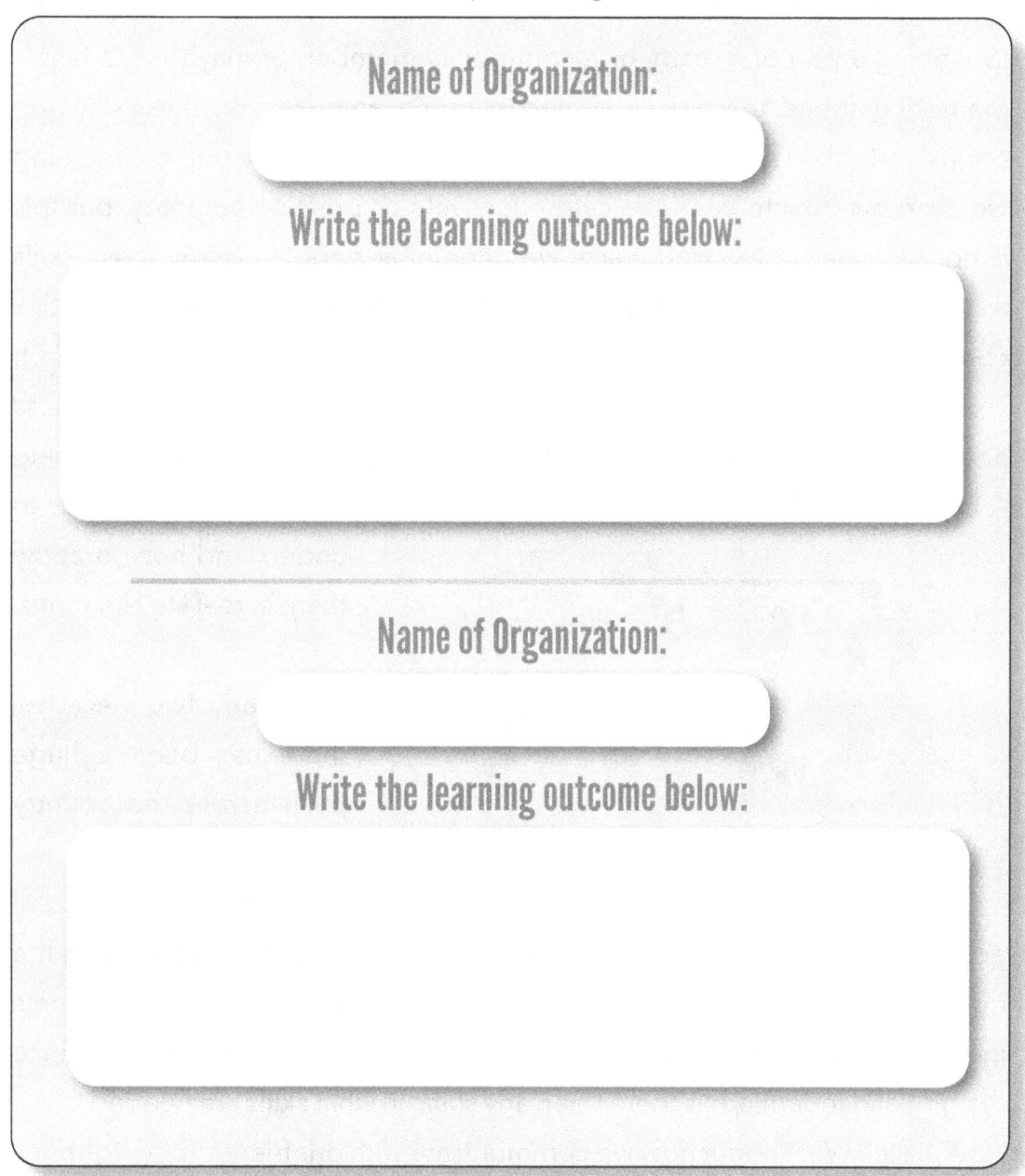

Name of Organization:

Write the learning outcome below:

Name of Organization:

Write the learning outcome below:

Why are Relationship Skills Important?

Why do we need to have relationship skills? The simple answer is, relationship skills are needed for us to be able to get along with others. Whether on the job, being a part of a team, or a community member, or maybe as a family member or friend, these skills are necessary. For some reason, these skills are often overlooked and taken for granted. We can run into the trap of assuming we all know how to communicate effectively or practice empathy, but this is not the case. In the workplace, we often hear people classify these skills as "soft skills" or "interpersonal skills". We use these skills to build positive connections with others where we show respect, empathy, and compassion. If you recall, we covered those three topics in our chapter on *Social Awareness* and also used them in the TREC Method. Being intentional and practicing

these skills will help us to understand how to apply them in real life situations.

For nearly two decades, there has been a huge push across the country to ensure students are prepared for a global economy. The demands and needs for a qualified workforce to take on the rigors and complexity of today's job is much different than what requirements may have been twenty years ago, or even five years ago. Think about it, since the global pandemic, has there been any shifts in what skills are needed in the workplace? What about how we communicate with our friends, or neighbors, and maybe even our family members? It's really interesting to see my elderly grandmother or my aunts communicate via FaceTime or Zoom. Did we ever think we would see such a quick shift in how we communicate? I remember seeing something similar to this in a Star Trek episode a few decades ago and thought, "Huh, that'll never happen in my lifetime." Of course, no one could've ever predicted how the pandemic would change our lives, but to know how quickly we adjusted our lives is phenomenal. But, even before the global crisis, there was already a shift in focus on what skills are needed in the 21st Century.

21st Century Skills

21st Century skills is a set of abilities created by business leaders, educators, researchers, and others, that help workers stay up to speed with the demands of today's ever-changing world. These skills are particularly essential in the Information Age, a world highly connected and requires us to be able to relate, interact, and interface with everyone. The following are considered 21st Century Skills:

1. Critical thinking
2. Creativity
3. Collaboration
4. Communication
5. Information literacy
6. Media literacy
7. Technology literacy
8. Flexibility
9. Leadership
10. Initiative
11. Productivity
12. Social skills (Stauffer, 2022)

The top four are called the 4 C's and categorized as learning skills. If you noticed, collaboration, communication, and social skills are three of the twelve skills.

Activity #3: Reflection (Group or Individual)

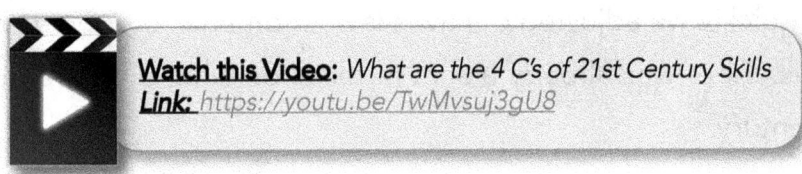

Watch this Video: *What are the 4 C's of 21st Century Skills*
Link: *https://youtu.be/TwMvsuj3gU8*

1. Why is developing collaboration skills so important?

2. Why do you think communication is difficult to master?

3. In what ways do you think critical thinking relates to self-efficacy?

COMMUNICATION

Effective communication is a core element to building positive relationships. Having clear communication doesn't just mean that a person is effective in how they use words to communicate an idea. It's really centered around understanding others and being willing to show respect and practice empathy. A major part of effective communication is also being an active listener. Active listening allows you to understand others and their situation better so that you can earn their trust and be able to actually help them.

There are two sides to communication within any relationship. While one side is speaking, the other side needs to be listening. If you're the one doing all the talking, you should use the 4-step structure to get the information you need and allow the recipient to understand your reasoning perfectly.

1. State what the conversation is going to be about. This might be discussing a problem or a potential plan for the future. This is where you can provide data, or facts and figures to back up your argument.
2. Provide information about how you fit in and what your motives are in having the conversation.
3. Explain the other person's intended role in the situation.
4. Discuss how you plan to reach your goal together.

This conversation structure will help keep your communication on track and you'll reach your goal more easily.

If you're the listener in the conversation, you'll need to practice active listening. This is more than simply keeping quiet while the other person is speaking. Make sure you really focus on the points the other person is making. Make eye contact regularly and even make notes if you can. Make sure you use verbal nods, (agreeing in the appropriate places) to encourage the other party and show that you are ready to work together.

The Pianist (Part 2)

The counselor called Linda's class and asked for her to join the meeting. Moments later, Linda entered the office and sat next to her mother in the counselor's office. The counselor began to explain to her how important it is to build strong relationships with others. "This will increase your chances of being employable in the global world that we now live in," the counselor said. "These are critical times to build those skills while you are still in high school." Linda's mother interrupted and shared that Linda has never had issues with others and she's not going to make her do something she doesn't want to do. The counselor understood, but then shared with Linda and her mother that though they could not force her to join a club, completing student service hours was a school requirement for graduation and she told Linda she would have to complete the hours in order to graduate the next year.

Linda was saddened when she heard this news and told her mother she would rather change schools than be forced to complete service hours and do things she had no motivation at all to do. Though Linda's mother wanted to support her daughter and thought Linda would actually learn a lot by volunteering her time helping others, she just didn't want to press the issue.

Activity #4: Make Recommendations (Group or Individual)

1. Discuss the core issues that the counselor and Linda's mother are faced with.

Issue #1

Issue #2

2. What two recommendations would you have for the counselor?

Recommendation #1:

Recommendation #2:

3. What two recommendations would you have for Linda's mother?

Recommendation #1:

Recommendation #2:

COLLABORATION (TEAM WORK)

Working together as a team is an important part of building successful relationships. A key element of being a team member is your willingness to engage with other members of your team and understanding that each of you brings a unique set of talents to the team.

It's vital that you spend some of the time connecting and understanding your goals. You should avoid taking on any task as a team without first setting some time aside to communicate. This time can be well spent getting to know one another and discussing how your individual efforts will serve the team. Appreciating your similarities outside the task is a great way to develop the friendship that your relationship will be based on.

Look at the other person's personal goals and what they want to get out of the project. They might have different goals than you, but that's fine. Make sure you find ways that your goals can fit together and be as mutually beneficial as possible. Appreciate the work that other people do. Take the time to look at how far you've come together. Your relationship will develop further, the more shared successes you have.

RESOLVING CONFLICT

You're always going to come across people that you don't particularly get along with, especially in work or educational environments. These are the people that you spend most of your time with, and they're picked by your school or company, not by you. The important thing to remember is that you must find some way to get along for the good of the rest of the people around you.

Try to reflect on the positive times that you've had together or successful projects that you've worked on. This will help you to see the good in everyone. Focus on goals that benefit both of you and try to share knowledge and expertise to work towards the same thing. It's also a good idea to look at yourself when trying to resolve conflict. Could it possibly be you that's causing some of the problem? Reflect on your actions and see if you can change your body language or communication to make your time together more positive.

SEEKING HELP

Remember that seeking help is nothing to be ashamed of, lots of relationships come off the rails occasionally and the most important thing is to recognize this and get back on track as soon as possible.

If you need help to resolve a conflict, then make sure you seek help from an impartial person. Don't ask your friend, as they're likely to side with you and that's likely to cause more of an issue.

Talk through the problems with the impartial party as a mediator. Talk about what your goals are and how you feel you're moving away from them. Consider your communication styles; do these need to change? Has the relationship broken down because the workload is just too much? Is it worth delegating or involving other people to remove the stress?

Remember, no one is going to criticize you for seeking help from others. But they might criticize if you don't deliver what you intended. Accept help whenever you can and form new relationships with those helpers along the way.

CHAPTER 5 PROJECT: THE PIANIST

Linda has a long conversation with her mother about the importance of building relationships, communication, and collaboration. Although Linda doesn't buy it totally, she does agree to think more about it. The next day, she sends this text to her mother:

If you are in a group setting, you should form a small group and discuss the TREC Method before completing the skit on the next page. The TREC Method is a great way to get your ideas on paper before using them in a scenario. Go through each line and answer each question. When you are finished, apply what you have learned throughout this chapter to the skit. There are no right or wrong answers here. I only recommend that you use the TREC Method as a guide to create your response. You will be pretending to be role-playing as Linda's mother. Also, enter sample dialogue that you might hear between Linda and her mother.

Write your responses directly into the dialogue bubbles. Each response should align with one of the four areas of the TREC Method. After you complete the guide, enter sample lines for both mother and daughter.

Discuss the TREC Method (Group or Individual)

Using the TREC Method to address the dilemma

What should Linda's mother be thinking about?

THINK:

What advice would you give Linda's mother to ensure she shows respect when addressing the problem?

RESPECT:

How would you advise Linda's mother to demonstrate empathy for others in this dilemma?

EMPATHY:

What are some ways in which you feel Linda's mother might show compassion?

COMPASSION:

After work, Linda's mother gives her a call. Use the TREC Method and write in sample dialogue for both characters.

CHAPTER 5 CHECKUP

1. Academic knowledge is a only form of education needed to succeed in today's world.   True ☐   False ☐

2. Which of the following are considered 21st Century Skills
    - ☐ Media literacy
    - ☐ Collaboration
    - ☐ Productivity
    - ☐ Critical thinking
    - ☐ Obedience

3. When you are not able to get along with others in the workplace or school, this is a sign of weakness and you should work to resolve issues.   True ☐   False ☐

4. Working together as a team is an important part of building healthy and successful _____ .

5. Give an example of collaborative work that you have been involved in.

CHAPTER 5 REFLECTION ACTIVITY FOR ECE EDUCATORS

Challenge your understanding of the Relationship Skills competency. Please read the vignette and answer the reflection questions at the bottom of the page.

3-year-old Kenneth sees his friend Mikah fall off the bike during outside play time. He runs over to Mikah and tries to help him up. Kenneth has seen his teachers do this. Kenneth is learning empathy and how to care for others and their feelings.

How could you as an adult who witnessed this share with Kenneth how he as applied some of the elements of the TREC Method in this scenario.

What are some ways in which you can use this incident as a teachable moment for other kids in your program or those you care for at home?

Chapter 6
Responsible Decision-Making

You are responsible for your own life choices.

The purpose of this chapter is to explore responsible decision-making and take a look at how we can make constructive choices that impact our lives and those around us in positive ways, and help children become more responsible decision-makers.

...what you will be able to do at the end of this chapter:

- identify problems in a scenario and take a responsible course of action to resolve the problem.
- analyze situations and determine how you can help solve a problem.
- make responsible decisions through role-playing.
- describe ways to make responsible decisions in a life-like situation.

...materials needed for this chapter:

- no additional materials are needed for this chapter.

There is never a wrong time to make the right decision.

Introduction: Responsible Decision-Making

When making decisions, we must consider all the potential consequences and think about how our choices will impact others. Responsible decision-making involves identifying a problem, exploring available options, evaluating how the decision will affect yourself and others, and considering ethical and moral obligations. Much of the work we've covered so far with other competencies has encouraged us to reflect on our emotions, regulate our behaviors, and connect with others. Now, we turn our focus to ways of making constructive decisions both individually and in groups.

By the end of the chapter, you will understand how to help children become more responsible decision-makers through personal reflections, group discussions, activities, analyzing a realistic scenario, and applying the TREC Method. This method will serve as a tool to guide you through real-world situations adults often face, helping you better support children in their development.

Jason's Story

Jason, a 10th grader at QuestVersity High School, was an aspiring basketball player. After being cut from the junior varsity team, he became depressed and struggled to accept the possibility of ending his basketball career. He had played basketball since he was four years old and didn't know how to break the news to his parents, who had supported him throughout the years. To avoid telling them, Jason began going to a local park with friends after school. Rumors circulated that some of his friends used vape pens. Jason confided in one friend that vaping helped him forget the pain of being cut from the team, even though he knew it was wrong.

One day, his mother picked him up from the back of the school and asked how practice went. Jason told her things were going well and pretended to be excited about being on the team. However, as she asked more questions, he responded with one-word answers, clearly avoiding the topic. Sensing something was off, she decided to bring it up with his father, hoping Jason might open up to him instead.

A few days later, Jason's mother received a progress report from the school and noticed that he had missed his 6th-period class for two straight weeks. She also saw that "basketball" was no longer listed for his 6th period; it had been replaced with "PE." Concerned, she called the attendance office, where they informed her that Jason had been switched out of the basketball class because he was no longer on the team. She left a voicemail with Jason's counselor, requesting a call back to discuss the situation.

When she picked Jason up from school that day, she asked him again, "How was practice?" Jason lowered his chin and mumbled, "It was okay." His mother took a deep sigh. Her heart was racing, but she decided not to confront him in the car.

Other background information:

- Jason was a popular student in middle school. He had a lot of friends and discovered interest in other things besides basketball. As a result, he stopped puttng in extra time outside of his scheduled practices to get better. Instead, he played video games with his friends and thought about becoming a game designer.

- Jason is the only child in his family.

Activity #1: Jason (Group or Individual)

1. What are main problems in this case?

2. What should Jason's parents be concerned about here?

3. Is anyone failing Jason in this case thus far?

4. What should Jason's parents do?

Text messages between Jason's mother and father

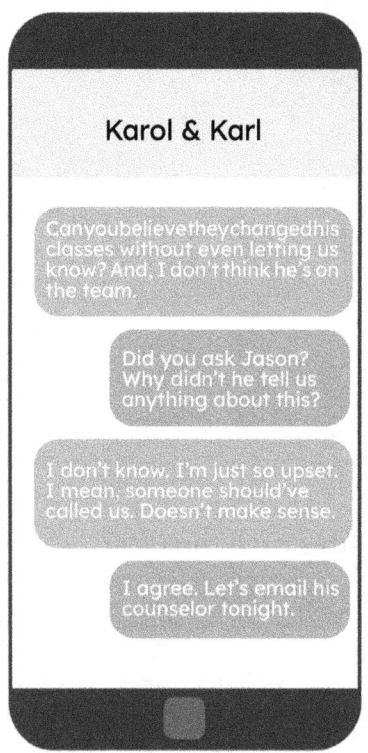

Karol & Karl

Canyoubelievetheychangedhis classes without even letting us know? And, I don't think he's on the team.

Did you ask Jason? Why didn't he tell us anything about this?

I don't know. I'm just so upset. I mean, someone should've called us. Doesn't make sense.

I agree. Let's email his counselor tonight.

5. Based on the text message exchanges, what else would you like to know?

Activity #2: Email to Counselor (Group or Individual)

Based on what you have learned about this case, write a short email message to Jason's counselor. You will take the role of Jason's parents. You will include the **Subject Heading** and a **Message**.

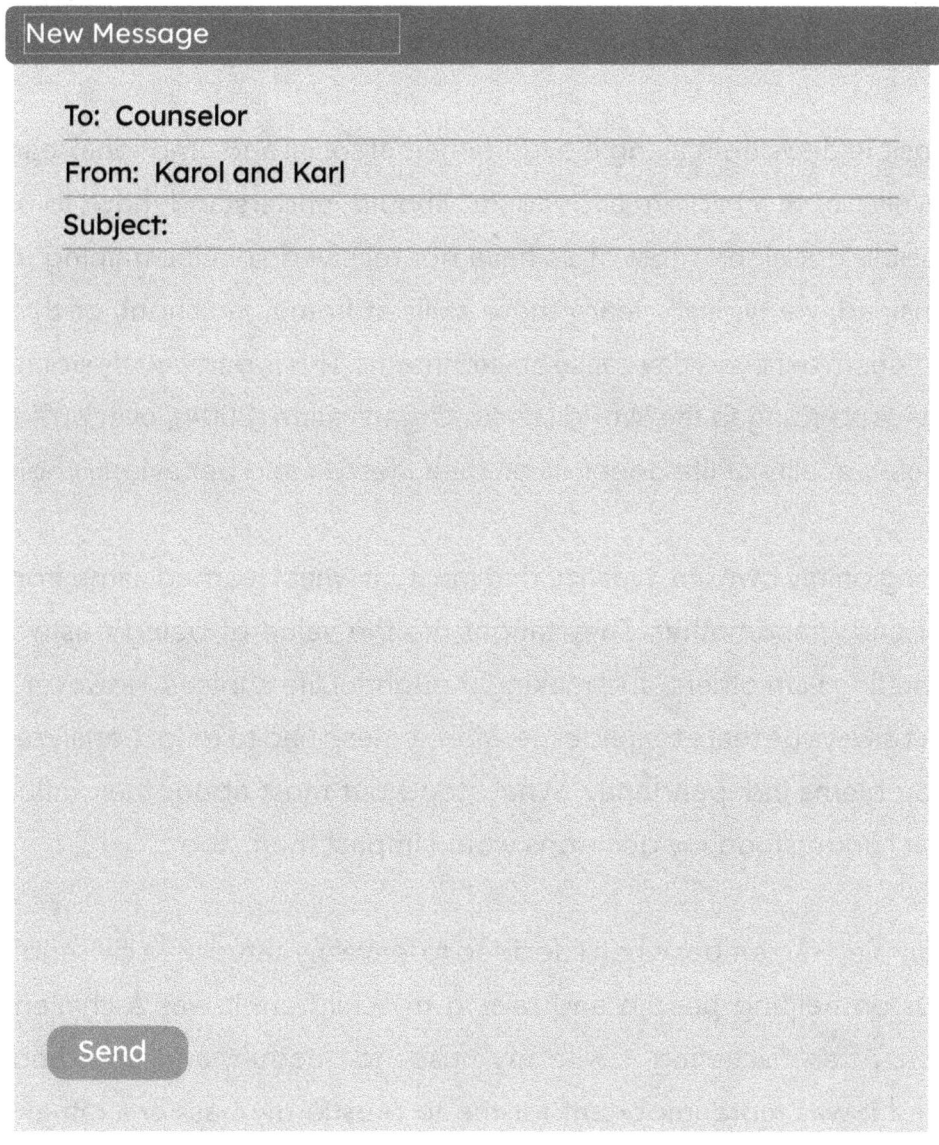

Responsible Decision-Making

Making the right decision begins with accurately defining the problem. This process often starts with self-reflection, which is crucial for understanding, meditating on, evaluating, and consciously considering our behaviors, desires, attitudes, and feelings. By practicing personal critique, we can better identify problems and make more informed decisions.

Responsible decision-making is a fundamental social and emotional learning skill. While both children and adults should understand how to make responsible decisions, most of us have not received specific training in this area. Instead, we typically learn these skills at home, in school, or through interactions in our everyday social environments. This is particularly significant because, according to the World Health Organization (2004), over 60% of an individual's quality of life depends on their lifestyle and behavioral choices.

Reflecting on my own life, I realize that much of what I learned came from my mother and grandmother. They taught me the value of being trustworthy, collaborating with others, and making thoughtful life choices. However, they couldn't always be there to guide me. Many times, I had to reflect, analyze, and solve problems independently. What stood out most about their influence was that I understood my decisions would impact them, too.

For example, I remember when I decided to leave my career as a civil engineer to focus on helping people and raising my children. It was a challenging decision. After discussing it with my husband, mother, and grandmother, I realized it was more important for me to pursue my passions rather than continue pretending to be happy as an engineer. However, this choice required careful consideration. I thought about the years I spent studying in college, the sacrifices my mother made to support me financially, and the resources invested in my education. These factors weighed heavily on me.

Ultimately, after thoughtful reflection and conversations with those closest to me, I decided to change careers. It turned out to be one of the best decisions I've ever made, and I have no regrets. Had I made this decision without consulting others, the transition would have been far more difficult. For instance, it wouldn't have been responsible to come home and announce to my husband and daughter, "Guess what? I quit today." Such a decision would have significantly affected my family in many ways.

Of course, my earning potential as an engineer was far greater than what I expected in my new path. However, the beauty of thinking through the problem was recognizing how my choices would affect those around me and ensuring my decisions aligned with my values and goals.

Activity #3: Big Decision (Group or Individual)

1. Discuss a time in your life when you had to make a big decision.

2. How did you go about making the decision? Did you include or consider others?

Jason (Part 2)

Jason's counselor called the next morning to express his concerns about Jason. He admitted that he should have notified Jason's parents about the class change but explained that the school had been focusing on helping students advocate for themselves. The counselor said, "I was clear with Jason that he needed to tell you about the class change. He was upset about being cut from the team and didn't know how to share it with you. He specifically asked me not to call you because he wanted to handle it himself. Since he has been responsible in the past, I felt this was something he could manage on his own."

The counselor also mentioned that Jason had been spending time with a few students known to go to the park during 6th period, where they had been seen smoking marijuana. "As far as I know, I haven't heard anything about Jason doing that, but I wanted to make you aware," he added. Jason's parents, however, disagreed with the school's decision to leave such a serious matter entirely to their son. They also didn't believe Jason would engage in drug use. Unsatisfied with the counselor's justification for not contacting them, they decided to call the principal and schedule a meeting.

Before meeting with the principal, Karol and Karl took the time to document the events leading up to the situation. They also sat down with Jason, urging him to be honest about ditching 6th period and addressing the rumors about going to the park and possibly using vape pens. Jason admitted to skipping class because he didn't know how to cope with being cut from the team but denied using any drugs.

The exchange is on the **next page.**

"I don't know what you guys are talking about. Just because I went to the park and some of the other kids might be using drugs, you think I'm using drugs too?" Jason said defensively.

Karol's eyes shifted to her husband. She hunched her shoulders and sighed. "I mean, what can we do?"

Karl took a deep breath and looked Jason directly in the eyes. "Son, we want to support you and make sure you're making good choices."

"I am, Dad," Jason pleaded, his face forming into a frown. He then turned to his mother. "What? You don't believe me?"

"We're not saying that, honey. It's just… we don't know. You're not on the team, and then you ditch class to go to the park…"

"That doesn't mean I use vape pens!" Jason said in an elevated tone.

"Okay. Forget about the vape pen thing," Karl interjected. "I've always told you not to use drugs, and I hope you're telling us the truth."

"But it doesn't help when you lied to me about being at practice when you weren't there. You just flat-out lied to me. How are we supposed to believe you? Now we're going to be meeting with the principal…"

"The principal?" Jason blurted, sucking in a sharp breath. "So, I'm in trouble? What are you going to meet with her about?"

"I want to know why they didn't tell us about changing your class," Karl replied.

Jason shook his head in frustration. "I'm not a baby."

Activity #3: Playing the Devil's Advocate (Group or Individual)

Karol and Karl have scheduled a meeting with the principal and the counselor. Prior to the meeting, they made sure to search the school's website and saw this as one of the schoolwide goals.

> *"Self-directed learners who can solve complex problems and advocate for their own educational and personal life experiences."*

1. What are some key points you think the principal might bring up in the meeting in relation to this goal?

Principal's Notes:

2. What are some key points you think the counselor might bring up in the meeting in relation to this goal?

Counselor's Notes:

IDENTIFYING AND ANALYZING THE PROBLEM

Before making a decision, particularly one that will impact others, it's important to first identify and analyze the problem. However, it's not practical to put significant time and effort into every single decision we make. For example, imagine spending hours deciding which brand of bottled water to drink. That would waste a lot of time. And that's just water—we'd have to do the same for every other choice, like the color of our socks or the shirt we want to wear. We'd quickly become overwhelmed with information.

When we talk about responsible decision-making, we're focusing on decisions that not only affect us but also impact others. In Jason's case, his decision not to tell his parents has led to additional choices that are compounding the problem and making matters worse. Moreover, his parents now have doubts about his honesty in other areas and are questioning one of the school's goals: to help all students become "self-directed learners who can solve complex problems and advocate for their own educational and personal life experiences."

Decision-making can be a stressful process. Often, we perceive seeking assistance as a sign of weakness and feel we must make decisions on our own. This approach is ineffective for two reasons:

- Deciding by yourself puts all the pressure of the outcome on you as an individual. Meaning that, if you happen to make a wrong decision you feel that you have to bear those consequences alone, which adds to your stress and can have serious effects on your mental wellbeing.

- It also means that you aren't considering the feelings or well-being of the others involved and, although the decision might work for you, it might affect others in ways that you hadn't thought of.

The best way to address both issues is to involve others in the decision-making process. Decisions become easier when they are shared. Seeking input from others allows you to consider their circumstances and opinions, enabling you to work toward a solution that benefits everyone.

BEHAVING ETHICALLY

You've identified what needs to happen and what's best for you and those around you. However, it's equally important to recognize your responsibility to act ethically. Take into account the social environment, the consequences for others involved, and how your decision might affect them. If your choice benefits you at the expense of others, ask yourself: is it truly an ethical decision?

Additionally, consider the safety of those around you. Are there risks or concerns for others if you proceed with your decision? Keep in mind that if your decision doesn't benefit everyone, it doesn't necessarily mean it's unethical. It can still be the right decision as long as it doesn't intentionally harm others or cause undue harm.

SOLVING THE PROBLEM

After identifying the problem, analyzing the situation and its impact on others, and considering the ethical aspects, you are ready to make a decision. Looking at Jason's situation, we can see how quickly problems can become complicated.

If you are in a group setting, form a small group and discuss the TREC Method before completing the dialogue on the next page. When you're finished, apply what you've learned throughout this chapter to the scenario. There are no right or wrong answers here—you'll be role-playing as a friend of Jason's parents.

Discuss the TREC Method (Group or Individual)

Using the TREC Method to address the dilemma

What should Linda's be thinking about?

THINK:

What advice would you give Linda's mother to ensure she shows respect when addressing the problem?

RESPECT:

How would you advise Linda's mother to demonstrate empathy for others in this dilemma?

EMPATHY:

What are some ways in which you feel Linda's mother might show compassion?

COMPASSION:

Write your responses directly into the dialogue bubbles. Each response should align with one of the four areas of the TREC Method. After you complete the guide, enter sample lines for Jason's parents and their friend (*played by you*).

After work, Jason's Parents call a Friend:

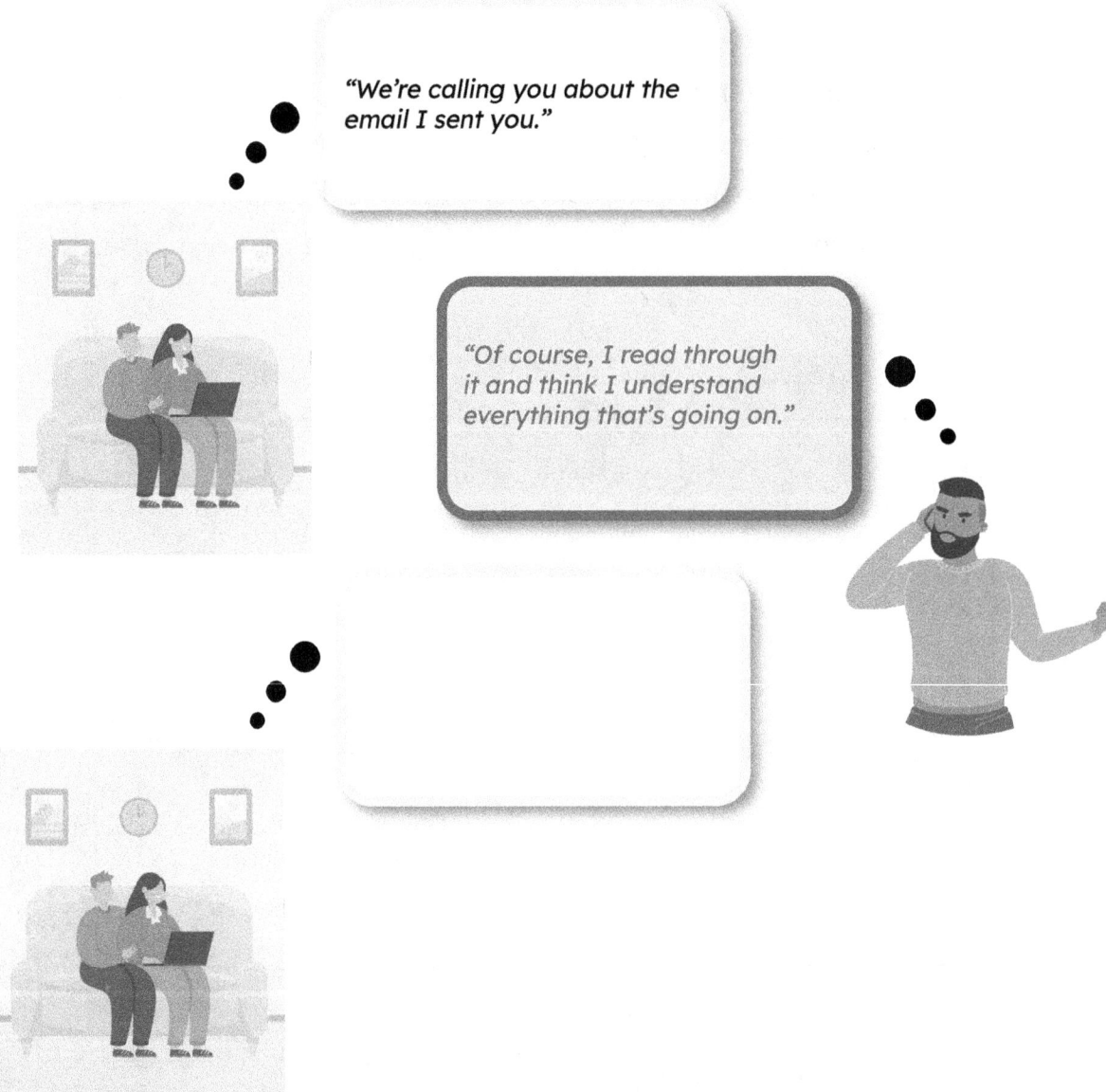

"We're calling you about the email I sent you."

"Of course, I read through it and think I understand everything that's going on."

CHAPTER 6 REFLECTION ACTIVITY FOR ECE EDUCATORS

Challenge your understanding of the Responsible Decision-Making competency. Please read the vignette and answer the reflection questions at the bottom of the page.

Kierra, age 4 is the youngest in her family and she has two older siblings, ages 7 and 10. Kierra attends preschool at the elementary school that her siblings attend. Kierra watches everything her brother and sister do and many times Kierra has a hard time making good choices. Kierra is playing with her friends Tiffany and Sage and they are playing a tag. Kierra is tagged and is out. Kierra has the choice to be mad or sit on the grass and wait until it's her turn again. Well, Kierra decides to call Sage and Tiffany very mean names, gets mad and storms off.

As you observed this happening, what are some of the first steps you would take to address Kierra's behavior?

Review Appendix B and list a strategy that you might use to help Kierra. You can also create one of your own. Why would you use this strategy?

*Please see Appendix B on strategies for the Responsible Decision-Making competency.

CONCLUSION

Congratulations! You have completed the "Why Social Emotional Learning Matters" journey. As stated at the beginning of this book, SEL matters because it helps us better understand ourselves and others, manage our emotions, set and achieve goals, and build positive relationships. First, we explored the importance of the "Whole Child," then we examined the Five Social Emotional Competencies: Self-Awareness, Self-Management, Social Awareness, Responsible Decision-Making, and Relationship Skills. Along the way, we learned tools and strategies to navigate challenging situations and foster social-emotional growth.

Remember, this is a marathon, not a sprint. Embedding these practices into our daily lives takes time, whether you are a parent, caretaker, coach, counselor, recreational worker, or play another role in the lives of children. Take it one day at a time, and focus on one competency at a time.

As the saying goes, "It's easier to build strong children than to repair broken adults." Every child brings something unique to the world, and we might just hold the key to unlocking their treasure. Above all, continue this important work guided by one of the most powerful words in any language: love.

FINAL ACTIVITY: complete the final project on the next page.

FINAL PROJECT: DIGITAL INFOGRAPHIC

Project: Digital Infographic
Time: 1 hour to 90 minutes
Delivery: Groups of 4 or 5. If taking the class online or at home, you can work on this independently.

INSTRUCTIONS:

In this project, you are going to create a digital infographic. You must include the following in your design:
- All five components of SEL covered in this book
- An image for each component
- A clear definition for each component
- An important piece of information to go with each component

You will share your design with the group at the end of this activity.

DO THIS: create a digital infographic that incorporates the five components of SEL. Please see Appendix A for easy-to-follow instruction on using a free online tool for creating your infographic.

Appendix A

Short Lesson on Creating an Infographic

An infographic is a visual representation that consists of images, charts, graphs, and a little text. They are excellent ways to convey information, educate, and inform. In today's world, filled with rich social media embedded with video, images, and colorful graphics, it's important that we get the attention of our intended viewers.

There are a lot of tools out there to create infographics. I chose to use Canva because it's a free online tool and has a lot of cool features. The features that we need to create a basic infographic are available in the free plan. You can create the infographic online using one of the many pre-built templates and download it to one of the common file types such as JPG, PNG, and PDF. This is perfect for what you need to do in this project.

Let's get started!!!

Step 1: Enter www.canva.com into your browser's address bar. You can create

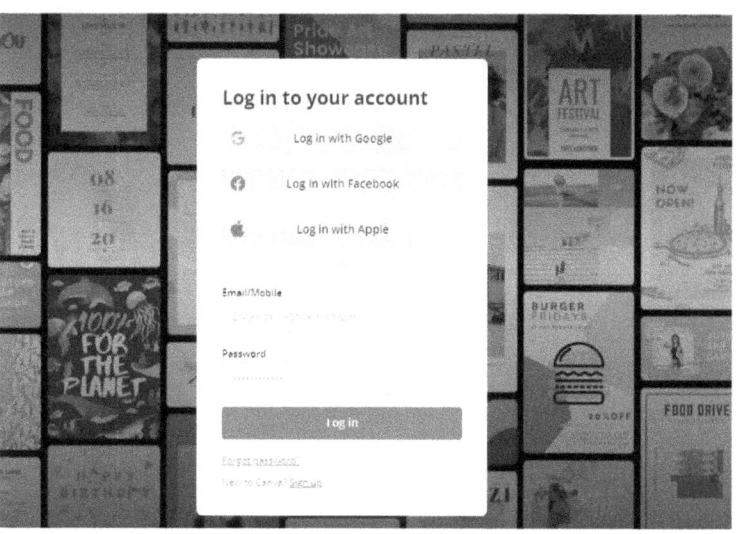

a new account or log in using your email account.

Step 2: Type "Infographic" into the search bar and select one of the design

Step 3: Edit the text and graphics. You can change color schemes, upload your own images, and a variety of other things to make your infographic look the way you want.

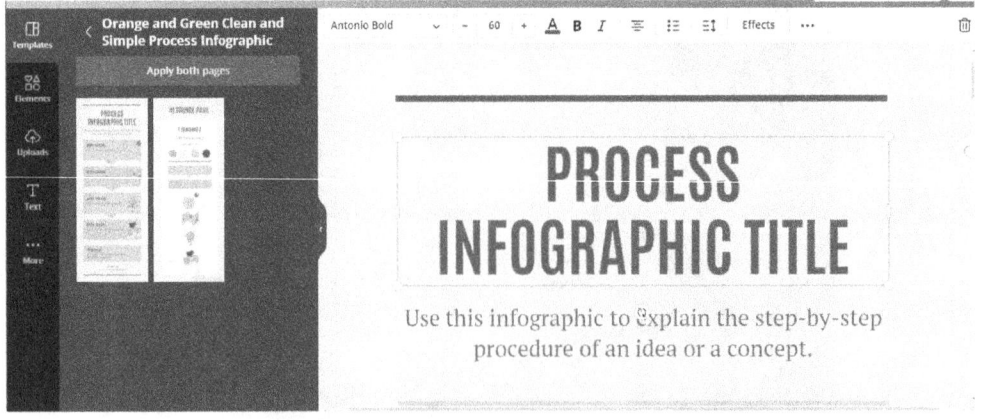

Step 4: After you have designed your infographic, you can now download it and share with others. Click the Download option at the top-right of the

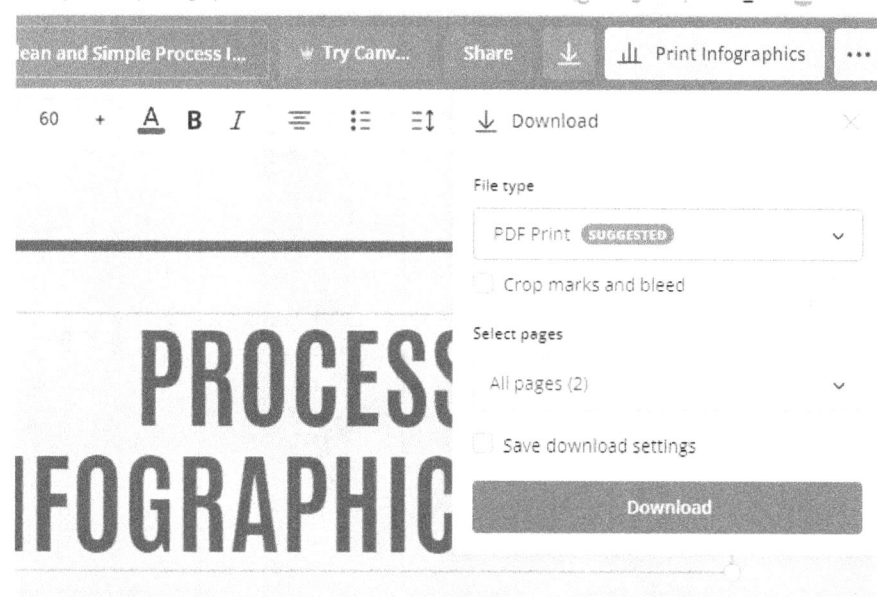

That's it!

Strategies for Building Social-Emotional Skills

Here are examples social-emotional learning strategies that can be used to help children build self-awareness,

Self-Awareness

Component	Strategy	Example Activity
Self-Awareness	**Journaling** is great for relieving stress and allows you time to focus on things that are important to you. You might ask yourself questions such as, "What made me happy today?" or "What should I do to prepare for tomorrow?"	• When working with a small group of young adults, an intervention counselor makes sure that each participant has a small notebook. This notebook is used to help develop a deeper understanding of one's inner-self. The counselor asks each participant to write down today's date at the top of an empty page and the following question, "What was a happy moment for me today?"
Self-Awareness	**Tracking your emotions** throughout the day. This is a wonderful way to discover how certain things affect your mood or emotions throughout the day.	• To help after-school students better track their emotions, a recreation director created a project where students cut and pasted clippings from magazines and newspapers that represented a particular emotion. After the first part of the project, she asked students to create a funny word to label each emotion. Lastly, they were asked to track each emotion for a week by logging the word, date, and time into their phones.
Self-Awareness	**Active listening** is about making the decision to not only hear what someone else is saying, but listening to the entire message they are trying to convey.	• When meeting with students, Dr. McMillan makes it a point to tell students he will be quiet and listen to what they have to say. Throughout the meeting, he often nods his head, pays attention to body language and tone, and uses responses such as "okay" and "uh-huh" to show that he's paying attention. He also uses paraphrasing techniques with sentence starters such as "So, what you're saying is..." or "let me make sure I'm getting this right..." or simply, "Got it" or "I understand".
Self-Awareness	**Self-reflection** allows us to think about our own thoughts and actions. Asking children to share how they view their performance on an activity requires them to self-reflect.	• After baseball games, Coach Teddy asks each player, "How did you get better today?" After the player's response, he affirms and validates the player's claim and always adds one or two other ways each player showed growth during the competition. This might include preparation, mental focus, attitude, etc. Dominique is adamant about her family having dinner together, especially on Sunday nights. During this time, she asks each person at the table, including visitors, "What were your highs and lows for the week?"

Self-Awareness

Component	Strategy	Example Activity
Self-Awareness	**Asking for feedback** on how your patterns of behavior might be impacting others. Honest feedback from others who want to see you grow and succeed is critical.	• Prior to a pre-season game, a little league baseball coach asked his former coach/mentor to watch a game and give him feedback in specific areas such as: team preparation, communication, game execution, etc. Additionally, he wanted to learned more about his personal strengths and weaknesses. He included these questions: 　• What did I do well since the last time you observed a game? 　• What two things can I do to have a positive impact on my team?
Self-Awareness	**Mindfulness practice** is a type of meditation that encourages you to get in control of your thoughts and feelings, slow down, and relax.	• A parent had received several calls from school about their child's anxiety prior to testing. The parents met with the teacher because they wanted to know how they could help their child succeed in class. The teacher offered some advice on "calming down" prior to taking exams by taking three deep breaths then saying "I'm going to do well on this test." The parents had noticed that the anxiety didn't start at school, but at home on days when tests were administered. The parents and teacher agreed that starting the exercise at home would be best.
Self-Awareness	*Write a strategy below…*	*Write an example that you have used or will use below…*

Component	Strategy	Example Activity
Self-Management	*Contracts* are great for setting expectations and they should give children a clear understanding of what they need to do to meet the conditions of the contract.	• Prior to the start of a new school year, the parents of a middle school student sat down with their child to write a contract. The contract included items such as study/homework time, chores, and incentives the child could earn if they met the conditions of the contract. The child was happy because he was involved in creating the contract and had a clear understanding of what his parents expected of him.
Self-Management	*Goal-setting* is a great way for children to create a plan with realistic steps to accomplish a goal. Goal-setting helps to develop a growth mindset.	• At the end of December, Dominique begins thinking about her goals for the upcoming year. One activity that she has done several years with her children is creating vision boards. She has a lot of fun finding images that represent ideas and concepts and pastes them to the poster board in the most creative ways. After doing it for several years, she has turned this into an activity with friends, and now that her children are young adults, they have vision board parties with their friends.
Self-Management	*Time management planning* is a way to plan your time throughout the day so that you can be more organized and accomplish more.	• A teacher realized that a lot of his 9th grade students needed help managing their time throughout the day. With so many students being involved in clubs and other after school activities, he found that many of his students weren't turning in assignments on time and keeping up with their weekly check-ins for a unit project they were working on. Instead of complaining and issuing students unsatisfactory grades, he decided to incorporate a daily planner into their assignments.
Self-Management	*Impulse control activities* are great for helping us resist certain behaviors or impulses that get in the way of accomplishing a particular goal.	• A preschool teacher noticed that every time she would transition to a new part of her lesson, one of her students would yell, "No. I don't want to do that." She discussed this with her student's parents and they shared that they experience the same thing at home. The teacher recommended a reward system that would encourage the child to resist the impulse to blurt out during class. She was aware that the student loved to play with Lego sets, she suggested this to the parents. "I want to create a reward system. I'll place three Lego blocks on my desk. Whenever Michael blurts out during class I'll take a block off of my desk. If there are any blocks remaining just before our free play time, he'll be able to use the free time to play with the Lego set for an extra five minutes."

Self-Management

Component	Strategy	Example Activity
Self-Management	**Behavior monitoring** is a great way to observe, record, and reflect on certain thoughts and behaviors with the goal of redirecting when necessary and holding ourselves accountable for our behaviors.	• Mr. Jones teaches art to elementary school-age children at a local community center on weekends. He began to realize that many of his students didn't screw the lids back on the small paint containers when they went on extended break, and even worse, when class was over. Initially, he didn't mind too much but after speaking to a staff member about purchasing additional paint, she replied, "Didn't we just purchase paint last week? There's no way you should be out of paint." Mr. Jones shared with her that students are leaving the lids off of the paint containers and this is drying up the paint and making it useless. He has told students on several occasions to be more responsible, but nothing has changed. The program manager recommended that he create a behavior monitoring tool with a goal, rule, and daily tally that each student could use to track their behavior of screwing the lids back on paint containers.
Self-Management	**Breaking assignments into bite sizes (Chunking)** is strategy used to increase motivation by breaking assignments into smaller pieces so that children (and adults) are able to accomplish smaller goals on their way to attaining bigger goals.	• Monique had been preparing her cheer team for a regional competition that would determine if they would qualify to participate in the national championship. One thing she had noticed when preparing her team for regionals, is that they became frustrated when they didn't complete the 2 minute and 30 second routine to perfection during practice. She started to hear moans of frustration and words of doubt, "We are horrible" one of her captains said, after an intense practice that left the team in an emotional quandary. Monique hadn't seen the team in such disarray since the start of the season. To boost their motivation, she decided to break the routine into 20 second intervals so that they could focus on smaller parts of the routine at a time.
Self-Management	*Write a strategy below...*	*Write an example that you have used or will use below...*
Self-Management	*Write a strategy below...*	*Write an example that you have used or will use below...*

Social-Awareness

Component	Strategy	Example Activity
Social-Awareness	**Teamwork** is a great way to practice positive communication with others and it helps with conflict resolution and cooperation.	• A high school teacher served as the club advisor at her school for several years. She noticed that the number of clubs had grown significantly in recent years but many of the student leaders didn't know each other and this often caused issues when trying to coordinate the yearly calendar and school-wide events. One year, she added a team-building activity to the leadership conference to build better camaraderie between students. She created a scavenger hunt where teams of student leaders worked together to explore clues around campus to solve a problem.
Social-Awareness	**Restorative circles** are great for allowing us to process and express our thoughts and feelings in a safe place, and resolve conflict in a more positive and constructive way.	• After Dr. McMillan was trained on restorative practices, one of the strategies he began implementing is restorative circles. In lieu of harsh, punitive measures for certain behaviors, he conducted restorative circles with students who were experiencing conflict. With parental consent, these circles allowed student to think and process their role in the conflict, own their behavior, think about how their actions might have harmed others, apologize, and agree to move forward on better terms.
Social-Awareness	**Building empathy** is an important strategy to help children actively listen and identify the emotions of others with the goal of being compassionate towards them.	• In order to get his team to demonstrate more compassion for each other, Coach B decided to do a fun activity with his team on a Saturday morning. He asked the players to bring in old magazines, newspapers, or images from the Internet. He broke the team into groups of five and passed out a several poster boards, markers, and scissors to each group. He then asked them to cut out images from the sources, group them, and post them on the poster boards under a title that best represented the expression shown in the image. Next, each group took turns sharing their images and the feeling words associated with the images. Finally, each group had to come up with three questions they would pose if they saw a teammate displaying a particular emotion.

Social-Awareness

Component	Strategy	Example Activity
Social-Awareness	**Respectful dialogue** is an engagement strategy that focuses on thoughtful, honest, and reflective conversations centered on understanding others better.	• Ms. Holley has been teaching history for several years. She loves for her students to engage in discourse because it helps them develop great communication skills. Since she incorporated debates into her curriculum, she has noticed that the skills learned has helped students beyond her classroom. When asked about how she teaches this skill, she shared that she closes a unit by drawing a "T" on the board with a topic above the "T", and then writes opposing positions on each side of the vertical line. Students are free to choose a side (she makes sure there is balance) and she gives her student 20 minutes to take notes and research the topic. Since they have already covered the content from the unit, it doesn't take them long to complete this part of the activity. She follows a 5-Step Debate format that she created for her class.
Social-Awareness	**Perspective taking** is a powerful strategy and social skill that encourages a person to consider a perspective from a point of view different from their own.	• Coach Tameca was excited about being hired as the new coach for the middle school softball team. She had learned so much from softball after years of playing throughout her childhood and also four years in college. During her meeting with the principal, she shared the importance of each player having the same gear and coming to practice daily with "clean" white pants. She was so adamant about uniformity that she said to the principal, "If a kid cannot follow team rules, they can't play for me." Though the principal was happy that she was knowledgeable of the game and had a lot of experience, she wasn't sure that the strict guidelines were acceptable and conducive to the type of caring and supportive environment they were trying to build. She simply asked the coach, "I want you to take the perspective of a family that might not have resources to clean their child's pants daily. What would you suggest?" Coach Tameca put some careful thought into her response.
Social-Awareness	*Write a strategy below...*	*Write an example that you have used or will use below...*

Relationship Skills

Component	Strategy	Example Activity
Relationship Skills	***Communication and collaboration*** strategies are great for getting children to work together for a common goal.	• Akil runs an after-school program in his local community. He was thinking of a project that would require his students to be involved in a community service project that focused on a particular cause. He had attended a high school volleyball game a year before and was excited to know that the team was bringing awareness to breast cancer by wearing pink socks, recognizing a local cancer survivor, and asking fans to wear something pink. Wanting to get his students involved, he contacted the school and asked if his program might collaborate with the school and provide some assistance. After a meeting with the school, Akil brought the information back to his students and decided to work on a plan with milestones that could help them manage the project. Roles were assigned and the students went to work on the posters.
Relationship Skills	***Building rapport*** is the process of establishing a connection with someone and building mutual trust.	• As a teacher, Dr. McMillan understood the importance of getting to know his students within the first couple of weeks of school year. Accepting that he was bad at remembering names, one of the first assignments he issued students was creating a name tent that would be placed on their desks. It listed their name, something unique about them, a hobby, and a goal. He also created a name tent and shared some things about himself. This was extremely useful because he was able to learn something about them. This made it easier to greet students in the morning, have conversations with them during lunch, and ask them about their hobbies or interests after returning to school on Monday mornings. Most importantly, he could greet them by first name.
Relationship Skills	***Conflict resolution*** is a strategy that focuses on bringing two or more parties together with the goal of finding a peaceful resolution to a problem.	• The parents of a middle school student noticed that their son had been withdrawn from social contact for a few weeks. He was typically talkative and got along with many kids at his school, and he was also a part of an after school club. Lately, he had been arriving home early from school and walked straight to his room. Concerned, the parents called one of his teachers. The teacher shared that he had also noticed some changes in his behavior and would have a conversation with him. After a short conversation with the student, the teacher discovered that he had gotten into an argument with a close friend over a broken gaming unit. The teacher offered a mediation session with both students to resolve the matter and he was confident he could get the students to a better place in their friendship.

Relationship Skills

Component	Strategy	Example Activity
Relationship Skills	**Peer teaching** is a strategy where help and support is administered by someone of equal status.	• A preschool teacher realized that the majority of her class was not progressing towards the goal of identifying shapes accurately. However, Parker, age 4, could identify all of the shapes and had already met the goal. Ms. Mikayla had recently attended a training and learned how to use peer teaching and role playing strategies in the classroom and was eager to implement them. Ms. Mikayla pulled out her beautiful hand cut felt shapes and a felt board. Parker sat on the floor in front of the class while Ms. Mikayla sat with the students in a circle. Parker played the role of the teacher, holding up the shapes and asking the class to name the shape she held up. Parker would first name the shape then call on a student to name the shape after her. All of the children were engaged in the activity and learned their shape in a short amount of time.
Relationship Skills	**Role playing** is a powerful strategy where someone assumes the role of someone else and engages in real-life situations.	• To introduce her volleyball club team to the social influences that shaped the world of professional sports, Coach Johnson wanted to give her players some background on the civil rights struggle prior to their visit to Dodger Stadium to honor the life of Jackie Robinson. When she first introduced the idea to the team, she wasn't sure how her players would respond. But, to her surprise, they were quite interested. The assignment was for them to work in pairs and write a one-page conversation between Branch Rickey and Jackie Robinson that might have occurred over a cup of coffee the night before Jackie Robinson played in his first game MLB game. She told them they would be role-playing and presenting their work to the team before the next practice.
Relationship Skills	*Write a strategy below...*	*Write an example that you have used or will use below...*

Responsible Decision-Making

Component	Strategy	Example Activity
Responsible Decision-Making	***Stop, think and analyze*** is a strategy that forces us to stop, think, and analyze a problem before acting on a situation. This is the first component of the TREC Method.	• Malcolm, a bubbly 5 year-old, arrived to Ms. Valarie's family day care excited to learn every morning. He was greeted by Ms. Valarie's assistant with a quick hello, but she said nothing to his father. She told Malcolm, "Hurry up. You are late to breakfast". Ms. Valarie noticed the interaction and felt that she was brash. She pulled her assistant to the side and asked, "Are you okay?" She responded with, "I'm just annoyed that he's late everyday and it's disruptive to our morning routine". Ms. Valarie reminded her to "stop, think, and analyze" before casting judgment. Valarie called Malcolm's father later that day to discuss the frequent tardiness issue. Malcolm's father shared that his work schedule was recently changed to the grave-yard shift and he tries his best to get Malcolm to school on time. He apologized for the situation. Valarie was understanding, but also shared how Malcolm being late disrupts the daily routine and how it affects Malcolm's learning. Malcolm's father shared that his schedule was temporary and will go back to normal in a week.
Responsible Decision-Making	***Help-seeking*** is a coping strategy where assistance is sought to help solve a particular problem.	• A program coordinator for a school district was given the assignment of finding qualified tutors for students who needed additional help with mathematics. Knowing there were limited funds to pay tutors, he reached out to the local university to see if there were ways for math majors to provide support to students at his district. While meeting with the Dean of the math department, he learned that there are students in an upper division, independent study course that might be able to incorporate the tutoring assignment into their project.

Responsible Decision-Making

Component	Strategy	Example Activity
Responsible Decision-Making	**Collaborative decision-making** is a strategy allows groups to analyze a problem, brainstorm possible solutions and consequences, build consensus, and make a decision.	• Carole worked for a community-based organization whose mission was to "provide art classes to kids in under-served urban communities" where she lived. She realized it would be a difficult endeavor that would require the voices and experience from many community stakeholders. Though she had a lot of experience developing and managing successful projects in the past, she understood the critical role community members played in the success of the program. She spent a considerable amount of time building relationships and forming a steering committee and an advisory board that would work collaboratively to support the program.
Responsible Decision-Making	**Role playing** is a powerful strategy where someone assumes the role of someone else and engages in real-life situations.	• To introduce her volleyball club team to the social influences that shaped the world of professional sports, Coach Johnson wanted to give her players some background on the civil rights struggle prior to their visit to Dodger Stadium to honor the life of Jackie Robinson. When she first introduced the idea to the team, she wasn't sure how her players would respond. But, to her surprise, they were quite interested. The assignment was for them to work in pairs and write a one-page conversation between Branch Rickey and Jackie Robinson that might have occurred over a cup of coffee the night before Jackie Robinson played in his first MLB game. She told them they would be role-playing and presenting their work to the team before the next practice.
Responsible Decision-Making	*Write a strategy below...*	*Write an example that you have used or will use below...*

References

Agolla, J.E & Ongori, H. (2009). *An assessment of academic stress among undergraduate students: The case of university of botswana.* Retrieved from https://www.researchgate.net/publication/209835751_An_assessment_of_academic_stress_among_undergraduate_students_The_case_of_University_of_Botswana

Allen, J, (1988). *Children's cognition of stressful events.* Retrieved from https://link.springer.com/article/10.1007/BF01622979#citeas

Álvarez-Bueno, C., Pesce, C., Cavero-Redondo, I., Sánchez-López, M., Garrido-Miguel, M., & Martínez-Vizcaíno, V. (2017). Academic Achievement and Physical Activity: A Meta-analysis. Pediatrics, 140(6), e20171498. https://doi.org/10.1542/peds.2017-1498

American Association of University Women. (2011). Crossing the line: Sexual harassment at school. Retrieved from December 23, 2019 https://www.aauw.org/files/2013/02/Crossing-the-Line-Sexual-Harassment-at-School.pdf.

American Psychological Association. (2012). *Stress in america: Our health at risk.* Retrieved from https://www.apa.org/news/press/releases/stress/2011/final-2011.pdf

Anila, M. M. (2016). *Mindfulness based stress reduction for reducing anxiety, enhancing self-control and improving academic performance among adolescent students.* Indian Journal of Positive Psychology,7 (4), 390-397

Balaguru, V., Sharma, J., & Waheed, W. (2013). Understanding the effectiveness of school-based interventions to prevent suicide: A realist review. Child and Adolescent Mental Health, 18, 131-139.

Basch, C. E. (2010, March). Healthier students are better learners: A missing link in school reforms to close the achievement gap. Retrieved from https://healthyschoolscampaign.org/wp-content/uploads/2017/03/A-Missing-Link-in-School-Reforms-to-Close-the-Achievement-Gap.pdf

Bitsko, R. H., Holbrook, J. R., Ghandour, R. M., Blumberg, S. J., Visser, S. N., Peou, R., & Walkup, J. T. (2018). Epidemiology and Impact of Health Care Provider-Diagnosed Anxiety and Depression Among US Children. Journal of developmental and behavioral pediatrics : JDBP, 39(5), 395–403. https://doi.org/10.1097/DBP.0000000000000571

Breslau, J. (2010, March). Health in childhood and adolescence and high school dropout: California dropout research project #17. Santa Barbara, CA: University of California. Retrieved from http://cdrp.ucsb.edu/dropouts/download.php?file=researchreport17.pdf

Cassidy, K., Franco, Y. & Meo, E., (2018) Preparation for Adulthood: A Teacher Inquiry Study for Facilitating Life Skills in Secondary Education in the United States, Journal of Educational Studies, 4 (1), 33 - 46

CASEL. (2022, August 3). Retrieved August 10, 2022, from https://casel.org/fundamentals-of-sel/what-is-the-casel-framework/

Centers for Disease Control and Prevention (2019) Prevalence of Childhood Obesity in the United States; Childhood Obesity facts. Retrieved 23 December from https://www.cdc.gov/obesity/data/childhood.html

Concordia University. (2016, August 24). For teens, feeling safe at school means increased academic success: Research shows the impact of student bullying, depression on classroom engagement. ScienceDaily. Retrieved December 23, 2019 from www.sciencedaily.com/releases/2016/08/160824135308.htm

Cree, R. A., Bitsko, R. H., Robinson, L. R., Holbrook, J. R., Danielson, M. L., Smith, C., Kaminski, J. W., Kenney, M. K., & Peacock, G. (2018). Health Care, Family, and Community Factors Associated with Mental, Behavioral, and Developmental Disorders and Poverty Among Children Aged 2-8 Years - U.S., 2016. MMWR. Morbidity and mortality weekly report, 67(50), 1377–1383. https://doi.org/10.15585/mmwr.mm6750a1

De Ridder, D., Lensvelt-Mulders, G., Finkenauer, C., Stok, F. M., & Baumeister, R. F. (2012). *Taking stock of self-control: a meta-analysis of how trait self-control relates to a wide range of behaviors.* Personality and Social Psychology Review.16, 76–99. doi: 10.1177/1088868311418749

DePaoli, J. L., Atwell, M. N., Bridgeland, J. M. & Shriver T. P. (2018) Respected Perspectives of Youth on High School & Social and Emotional Learning, A Report for CASEL By Civic with Hart Research Associates, Retrieved December 23 2019 from https://casel.org/wp-content/uploads/2018/11/Respected.pdf

Doran, G. (1981). *There's a s.m.a.r.t. way to write management's goals and objectives.* Retrieved from https://community.mis.temple.edu/mis0855002fall2015/files/2015/10/S.M.A.R.T-Way-Management-Review.pdf

Dotson, R. (2016). *Does goal setting with elementary students impact reading growth?* Retrieved From *https://www.proquest.com/docview/1767793272*

Duckworth, A., & Yeager, D. S. (2015). Measurement Matters: Assessing Personal Qualities Other Than Cognitive Ability for Educational Purposes. Educational Researcher, 44(4), 237–251. https://doi.org/10.3102/0013189X15584327

Duckworth, A., Gollwitzer, P., Oettingen, G., Loew, B., & Grant, H. (n.d.). *Self-Regulation strategies improve self-discipline in adolescents: Benefits of mental contrasting and implementation intentions.* Taylor & Francis. Retrieved August 20, 2022, from https://www.tandfonline.com/doi/abs/10.1080/01443410.2010.506003

Duszka, C.D. (2015). The Effects of School Safety on School Performance. Retrieved from https://www.semanticscholar.org/paper/The-Effects-of-School-Safety-on-School-Performance-Duszka/97ee1b81ef16b3dc01473b921a32a2e42aec4dc0.

Dweck, C. S. (2008). Mindset: the new psychology of success. Ballantine Books trade pbk. ed. New York: Ballantine Books.

Ekanem, R.S., Apebende, E.U. & Ekefre, E.Y. (2011). Learning Environment And Pupils Academic Performance: Implications For Counseling, African Journals Online, 29 (1) 2011

FCUSD. (2022). Retrieved from https://www.fcusd.org/domain/1636

Feeding America (2019) Hunger in America, Retrieved 22 December, 2019 from https://www.feedingamerica.org/hunger-in-america/facts

Foster, J, Yaoyuneyong, G (2016). Teaching innovation: equipping students to overcome real-world challenges, Higher Education Pedagogies, 1:1, 42-56, DOI: 10.1080/23752696.2015.1134195

Garcia, E. & Weiss, E. (2016). Making whole child education the norm; How research and policy initiatives can make social and emotional skills a focal point of children's education, Economic Policy Institute Report. Retrieved 23 December, 2019 from https://www.epi.org/publication/making-whole-child-education-the-norm/

Gould, M. S., Lake, A. M., Kleinman, M., Galfalvy, H., Chowdhury, S., & Madnick, A. (2018). Exposure to Suicide in High Schools: Impact on Serious Suicidal Ideation/Behavior, Depression, Maladaptive Coping Strategies, and Attitudes toward Help-Seeking. International journal of environmental research and public health, 15(3), 455. doi:10.3390/ijerph15030455

Heckman, J., Pinto, R., & Savelyev, P. (n.d.). *Understanding the mechanisms through which an influential early childhood program boosted adult outcomes.* American Economic Review. Retrieved August 7, 2022, from https://www.aeaweb.org/articles?id=10.1257%2Faer.103.6.2052

Hofmann, W., Baumeister, R. F., Förster, G., & Vohs, K. D. (2012). *Everyday temptations: An experience sampling study of desire, conflict, and self-control.* Journal of Personality and Social Psychology, 102, 1318–1335

Jimenez, M. E., Wade, R., Jr, Lin, Y., Morrow, L. M., & Reichman, N. E. (2016). Adverse Experiences in Early Childhood and Kindergarten Outcomes. *Pediatrics*, 137(2), e20151839. doi:10.1542/peds.2015-1839

Kadiyono, A. L., & Hafiar, H. (n.d.). *The role of academic self-management in improving.* Retrieved August 20, 2022, from https://moam.info/the-role-of-academic-self-management-in-improving_5c4e5ebe097c47506d8b45ea.html

Kerr, D.C.R., Reinke, W.M., Eddy, J.M. (2013) Trajectories of depressive symptoms and externalizing behaviors across adolescence: associations with histories of suicide attempt and ideation in early adulthood. Suicide and Life Threatening Behavior, 43, 50-66

Kutsyuruba, Benjamin & Klinger, Don & Hussain, Alicia. (2015). Relationships among school climate, school safety, and student achievement and well-being: a review of the literature. Review of Education. 3. 103-135. 10.1002/rev3.3043.

Kweon, B.-S., Ellis, C. D., Lee, J.; Jacobs, K. (2017, February 3). *The link between school environments and student academic performance. Urban Forestry.* Urban Greening. Retrieved August 7, 2022, from https://www.sciencedirect.com/science/article/abs/pii/S1618866716300140?via%3Dihub

Lacoe, J. (2020). Too Scared to Learn? The Academic Consequences of Feeling Unsafe in the Classroom. Urban Education, 55(10), 1385–1418. https://doi.org/10.1177/0042085916674059

Lippman, L. H., Ryberg, R., Carney, R., & Moore, K. A. (n.d.). Key "soft skills" that foster youth workforce success: Toward a consensus across fields. Youth Power. Retrieved August 7, 2022, from https://www.youthpower.org/resources/key-soft-skills-foster-youth-workforce-success-toward-consensus-across-fields-1

Lynch, D. (1990). *Teaching students to be internally motivated.* Retrieved from https://www.proquest.com/openview/67ad79541386d811fc227aac4850348d/1?pq-origsite=gscholar&cbl=2030479

Malone, D (2019) *Applying social and emotional learning (SEL) in your classroom.* Retrieved https://blog.edgenuity.com/sel-and-self-management/

McMillan, D. T.(2018). *A single case study exploring self-efficacy in an after-school program.* (Doctoral dissertation). Retrieved from https://scholarcommons.sc.edu/etd/5049

Mental health in childhood: Undiagnosed and silently suffering. Child Focus. (n.d.). Retrieved August 7, 2022, from https://www.child-focus.org/news/mental-health-in-childhood-undiagnosed-and-silently-suffering/

Moffitt, T., Arseneault, L., Belsky, D., & Avshalom, C. (2010). *A gradient of childhood self-control predicts health, wealth, and public safety.* Retrieved from https://doi.org/10.1073/pnas.1010076108

Moreira, P.A.S., Dias, A., Matias, C., Castro, J., Gaspar, T. & Oliveira, J. (2018) School effects on students' engagement with school: Academic performance moderates the effect of school support for learning on students' engagement, Learning and Individual Differences, 67, 67-77.

Neff, K. (2015). *Self compassion: The proven power of kind to yourself.* William Morrow Paperbacks.

Payne, A.A., (2018). Creating and Sustaining a Positive and Communal School Climate: Contemporary Research, Present Obstacles, and Future Directions, National Institute of Justice, Retrieved 23 December, 2019 from https://www.ncjrs.gov/pdffiles1/nij/250209.pdf.

Plante, I., O'Keefe, P., & Theoret, M. (2013). *The relation between achievement goal and expectancy-value theories in predicting achievement-related outcomes: A test of four theoretical conceptions.* Retrieved from https://link.springer.com/article/10.1007/s11031-012-9282-9

Robbins, S. B., Lauver, K., Le, H., Davis, D., Langley, R., & Carlstrom, A. (2004). *Do psychosocial and study skill factors predict college outcomes? A meta-analysis.* Psychol. Bull. 130, 261–288. doi: 10.1037/0033-2909.130.2.261

Rodriguez-Fernandez, A., Ramos-Diaz, E., Axpe-Saez, I (2017). The Role of Resilience and Psychological Well-Being in School Engagement and Perceived Academic Performance: An Exploratory Model to Improve Academic Achievement, Health and Academic Achievement, Blandina Bernal-Morales, IntechOpen, DOI: 10.5772/intechopen.73580 Retrieved from December 23, 2019, from https://www.intechopen.com/books/health-and-academic-achievement/the-role-of-resilience-and-psychological-well-being-in-school-engagement-and-perceived-academic-perf

Saeed, S., & Zyngier, D. (2012). How motivation influences student engagement: A qualitative case study. Retrieved from https://files.eric.ed.gov/fulltext/EJ1081372.pdf

SAUSD. (2022). Retrieved from https://www.sausd.us/domain/2402

Shoda, Y., Mischel, W., & Peake, P. K. (1990). *Predicting adolescent cognitive and self-regulatory competencies from preschool delay of gratification: Identifying diagnostic conditions.* Developmental Psychology, 26(6), 978–986. https://doi.org/10.1037/0012-1649.26.6.978

Srivastava, S., & Angelo, K. M. (2009). Optimism, effects on relationships. In H. T. Reiand S. K. Sprecher (Eds.), *Encyclopedia of human relationships.* Thousand Oaks, CA: Sage.

Stauffer, B. (2022). *21st Century Skills.* Retrieved from https://www.aeseducation.com/blog/what-are-21st-century-skills

Tangney, J. B., Boone, A., & Baumeister, R. (2018, January 19). *High self-control predicts good adjustment.* Taylor & Francis Group.

Vohs, K. D., Finkenauer, C., & Baumeister, R. F. (2011). The Sum of Friends' and Lovers' Self-Control Scores Predicts Relationship Quality. *Social Psychological and Personality Science,* 2(2), 138–145. https://doi.org/10.1177/1948550610385710

WebMD. (2017). Retrieved from https://www.webmd.com/children/news/20150817/stress-survey

Whole Child Education (n.d.). Retrieved October 9, 2022, from http://www.wholechildeducation.org/about/

Yazzie-Mintz, E. (2010). Charting the path from engagement to achievement: A report on the 2009 high school survey of student engagement. Bloomington, IN: Center for Evaluation & Education Policy. Retrieved from http://ceep.indiana.edu/hssse/images/HSSSE_2010_Report.pdf

Zahn-Waxler, C., M. Radke-Yarrow, and R. A. King. 1979. Child rearing and children's prosocial initiations toward victims of distress." Child Development 50: 319-330.

Zimmerman, B., & Martinez-Pons, M (1988). *Construct validation of a strategy model of student self-regulated learning.* Journal of Educational Psychology 80(3), 284-290. Retrieved from https://www.researchgate.net/publication/232550661_Construct_Validation_of_a_Strategy_Model_of_Student_Self-Regulated_Learning

www.ingramcontent.com/pod-product-compliance
Lightning Source LLC
Chambersburg PA
CBHW080339170426
43194CB00014B/2620